Leading
& Managing
a Growing
Church

George G. Hunter III

Leading & Managing a Growing Church

ABINGDON PRESS / NASHVILLE

LEADING AND MANAGING A GROWING CHURCH

This book is printed on acid-free paper.

Library of Congress Cataloging-in-Publication Data

Hunter, George G.
    Leading & managing a growing church / George G. Hunter, III.
        p. cm.
    ISBN 0-687-02425-0 (alk. paper)
    1. Church growth. 2. Church management. I. Title: Leading and managing a growing church. II. Title.

BV652.25 .H845 2000
253—dc21

                                                    00-055830

00 01 02 03 04 05 06 07 08 09—10 9 8 7 6 5 4 3 2 1

MANUFACTURED IN THE UNITED STATES OF AMERICA

To the late Joseph D. Quillian, Jr.
Dean Emeritus,
Perkins School of Theology,
Southern Methodist University

Contents

Preface

In the 1990s, many church leaders reflected upon the reality behind Dietrich Bonhoeffer's observation that "The rusty swords of the old world are powerless to combat the evils of today and tomorrow." That comment, written a half century ago, now seems prophetic as we observe the changing populations the Church is called to reach. My books *How to Reach Secular People* (Abingdon, 1992) and *The Celtic Way of Evangelism: How Christianity Can Reach the West . . . Again* (Abingdon, 2000) unpacked some of the ways that the changing harvest, "secular" and even "neo-barbarian," can be reached and helped into Christian faith.

Bonhoeffer's prophecy haunted us even more as we observed more and more traditional churches that were unable to reach and retain the receptive, searching, secular people in their ministry areas, or even retain a bare majority of their own young people. Different, more "apostolic" ways of "doing church" were emerging in a few places that demonstrated the way forward in most places. My book *Church for the Unchurched* (Abingdon, 1996) explained what traditional churches could learn from the more pioneering churches if they wanted to move "from tradition to mission."

In the 1990s, we also began to face the formidable challenge of "transitioning" a traditional church for greater effectiveness in a changing culture. As church leaders labored to sell their people on "doing church" by a cultural relevance, small groups, and lay ministries kind of paradigm, they rediscovered Machiavelli's warning from the title page of *The Prince:* "There is nothing more difficult to take in hand, more perilous to conduct, or more uncertain in its success, than to take the lead in the introduction of a new order of things."

9

An unprecedented number of reflective church leaders rose to this formidable challenge. Beginning with Lyle Schaller's *Strategies for Change* (Abingdon, 1993), more good books were written on leading and managing change in churches than in all prior decades combined. Every such book, however, seemed to be predicated on one false assumption. They assumed that the pastors and other people who want to lead and manage change already know how to lead and manage! That assumption is not usually valid; many, indeed, haven't a clue.

This book provides "the missing link." This book delineates the management lore that most of the "leading change" books take for granted, without duplicating any of their models. This book will demonstrate, however, that the process of providing "management leadership" for an organization provides its own proven paradigm for leading and managing a changing organization. Furthermore, the last chapter focuses the book's management lore on the "Breakthrough Project" model for managing change, and even turnaround, in organizations. This model has been intuitively practiced in many "turnaround" churches but, to my knowledge, has not yet been commended to other churches in print.

The reader will notice that this book gathers momentum slowly, devoting the first four chapters to helping resistant Christian leaders get on board with the management principles that are unpacked in chapters 5 through 9. Chapter 10 offers a new method for managing "turnaround" in declining churches. A "Congregational Health Questionnaire" is provided as an appendix; church leaders have permission to photocopy it to assess their congregation's effectiveness around seven themes that relate to ministry, church growth, and leadership.

This book is written with gratitude for the thinkers, beginning with Peter Drucker, who produced the "management revolution" in the second half of the twentieth century. This book is written with the confidence that the best days of the Christian movement, even in "secular" North America and Europe, are ahead of us if we love "the Lord of the Harvest" with our minds as well as our hearts.

Chapter One: Why Any Church Leader Needs to Know the Principles of Management

The world's largest church is the Yoido Central Full Gospel Church of Seoul, Korea. Its membership, by April of 1998, was 734,309 members! The church, under the leadership of Dr. David (formerly Paul, before a name change) Yonggi Cho, has pioneered for a generation in both quantity and quality church growth. Virtually every member is active in one of the church's 25,051 "home cell groups"—groups of five to ten or more households which meet weekly to fulfill four agendas: prayer, ministry to each other, reaching pre-Christian people, and starting more cell groups! As each cell group reaches pre-Christian families, and as cell groups start new cell groups to reach pre-Christian families, the church continues to grow by more than 20,000 members per year.

An awesome organization of leaders supports this expanding church. Each of the 25,051 home cell groups has a leader, and an assistant leader (who is being groomed to start a new home cell group). An organization chart (if we could draw one) would show a network of bridges from the director of the pastoral care department to 21 district leaders, to 335 subdistrict leaders, to

2,500 section leaders, to the 25,051 home cell group leaders and as many assistant leaders. If my math is still with me, this church deploys 53,959 leaders in the pastoral care department of the church's organization! We are struck, again, by the magnitude of the church's organization when we learn that the church has 663 pastors, 64,457 deaconesses, 25,211 deacons, and 1,253 elders, and supports the work of 825 missionaries serving in 53 countries! The church reports a total of 145,052 leaders, essentially one leader for every five members.[1]

Dr. David Cho, senior minister of Yoido church, is, of necessity, an omnicompetent "leader" and "manager." His pulpit, no matter how strong, could never by itself generate such growth. Though Dr. Cho is a clear and magnetic preacher, his greatest gifts are in management and leadership, and thousands of other leaders in Yoido church are making their contribution primarily through effective management and leadership. We speak of management, here, not in the technical sense of "running a business" but in the generic sense of *"getting things done through other people"*[2] or "achieving the organization's objectives through other people,"[3] or "the process of working with and through individuals and groups and other resources (such as equipment, capital, and technology) to accomplish organizational goals."[4]

If the challenge of management is achieving the organization's goals through other people, then effective management is needed in most churches; the need is not limited to the Yoido super-church and other mega-churches. (Actually, their effective management of Yoido church substantially explains how the church grew; no church mysteriously attains "mega-church" size and then suddenly needs effective management!) Indeed, any full-time pastor whose church has more than 12 groups,[5] and whose worship attendance averages much more than 150, rediscovers his or her limitations. An industrious pastor, willing to court burnout, may shepherd a church averaging 200 in attendance. However, every shepherd is limited in the number of "flocks" and "sheep" he or she can care for without losing some sheep and seeing others run wild.

Lyle Schaller has contended for years that a "shepherd" must learn to become a "rancher" if a church is to grow much past 150 to 200 in attendance and, say, a dozen groups. In *Growing Plans*, Schaller explains that a church growth effort to move a church past middle size necessarily involves a fundamental change in the senior pastor's role and expectations:

> This effort can be reinforced if the senior minister's basic role is seen not as being a shepherd spending most of the day with one flock and considerable time with individual sheep, but as being a rancher. . . . The responsibility of the rancher . . . is to see the total picture, to make sure that everything gets done, rather than attempt to do all the work singlehandedly. Most important of all, the rancher['s] . . . responsibility is to delegate to others and to trust the people to whom specific responsibilities have been delegated. . . . The senior minister's own image of the role . . . can be very influential in determining whether the congregational leaders see their church as one big family or as a large and complex organization.[6]

In churches that have broken through the "200 barrier," the senior pastor still does shepherding but no longer pretends to shepherd everyone; most of the shepherding is now done through other people. (Often, the pastor shepherds the other shepherds.)

Furthermore, the effectiveness of other church staff people, and of many key lay volunteer leaders, depends on their management competence. For instance, the effective music director will get most of the singing and instrumental accompaniment done through others, and the Sunday church school superintendent will not be teaching all sixteen classes; she or he gets most of the teaching done through other people. The Charles E. Fuller Institute's old seminar "How to Break the 200 Barrier" once scratched where many church leaders continue to itch. You help the church to grow past this natural plateau of 200 by becoming a manager of ministries, that is, by getting the shepherding, and much of the other ministry, done through other people.

Carl George, former director of the Fuller Institute, demonstrates that the management challenge is also key to breaking the 400 and 800 barriers that growing churches typically experience. In *How to Break Growth Barriers*, George describes how most pastors begin their professional ministry as the shepherding pastors of small congregations. The small church pastor calls on people, prays for people, cares for people, and attends every meeting as the omnipresent, always available, chaplain of the faithful. Such a pastor experiences a period of euphoric vocational satisfaction from being so needed and so obviously useful. This euphoria fades as the pastor now serves about as many people as one shepherd can shepherd, as growth levels off, as some people leave, as the pastor's family wants more time, as the pastor gets in touch with burnout and the inability to meet everyone's expectations. In contrast to the typical shepherd, George profiles the rancher as one who refuses to cultivate dependency upon the pastor, gets people in ministry with each other, creates roles for other people, focuses on outcomes and the big picture, and pays the price to acquire "managerial skills."[7]

Carl George acknowledges that the specific shape of the pastor-manager's challenge will change from one numerical barrier to another. To break the 200 barrier, the three keys are to move the pastor from the shepherd to the rancher orientation, to move the church from a one-cell to a multi-cell structure, and to prepare laity for ministry and leadership, while guarding against the "small church mentality" creeping back in.[8] Breaking the 400 barrier involves greater attention to staff selection, and to delegation, and a changing role for the board. Planning and administration now shift from the board to the staff, with the board authorizing policy, selecting senior staff, approving budgets, and giving oversight.[9] Breaking the 800 barrier will typically involve the management of multiple worship services, specialized ministries and niche marketing, distinct ministries for three or four generations, and more intentionally and comprehensively organized lay ministries and small groups, with the need to recruit and develop more exceptional talent than the growing church needed in its earlier growth phases.[10]

Unfortunately, most people in church vocations who want their church to grow do not ordinarily think of themselves as "managers." They have several conscious roles, but "manager" is not one of them. I know pastors, infected by the "antibusiness" bias of some schools of theology, who respond to the suggestion of a "manager" role as they would to an obscenity! I know second-career pastors, who were effective senior managers of, say, a Sears store or a middle school in their first career, who assume that those early years were a "waste" and that nothing once learned about managing a hospital is useful in leading a church! In their defense, most divinity schools prepare people only for the shepherding role and not for the ranching role; furthermore, seminaries usually share the higher education academy's elitist scorn for the "business" culture.

Well, if you are the pastor, and you are doing *all* of the preaching, and teaching, and counseling, and visiting, and hospital ministry, and determining the budget, and deciding what color to paint the parlor, and doing everything else yourself, then indeed you are not a manager; you are only a practitioner. If, however, some of the

17

church's actions—teaching Sunday school, singing in the choir, chairing the women's meeting, or even typing the bulletin—are done by other people, you are also a manager. With enough experience and reflection, many church leaders ultimately decide that exercising the management role is necessary to get the work done and to empower the laity for their apostolic and priestly roles. Many church leaders also discover that learning to "get things done through other people" liberates them from the compulsive work addiction and burnout that are epidemic in the ranks of church leaders and frees more time and energy for relationships, innovation, recreation, study, prayer, and ministry. And, in time, a leader experiences even more satisfaction from helping someone else to perform a ministry than from doing it himself or herself.

In the late 1960s, I became a protégé of England's Lord Donald Soper. In addition to preaching at the Kingsway Hall Methodist Church in London, Soper was superintendent of the West London Methodist Mission—which then included more extensive social service ministries and institutions than any other church in Great Britain. The church's stationery listed the following ministries:

Kingsway Creche—for children
St. Luke's House—for men alcoholics
Stirling Court and Argyll House—"Second Stage
    Houses" for men alcoholics
St. Mary's House—for women alcoholics
Grove House—for unmarried expectant mothers
Alfred Hartley House—for old ladies
Emerson Bainbridge House—residence for
    young people
Goodliffe House—residence for retired men and women
Fellowship House—residence for young people
Hopedine—for unmarried mothers and their babies

Katherine Price Hughes Hostel—for girls in need of care
and supervision
WLM Clothing Store—a shop for those with little money

The mission staff and laity also engaged in many other
ministries outside of the institutions—such as prison
ministries, job placement, and work among prostitutes
and drug addicts. Soper spoke in the open air forums of
Tower Hill on Wednesdays and Speaker's Corner in
Hyde Park on Sundays, and he devoted many Tuesdays
as an active member of Great Britain's House of Lords.
In the thick of this career, Soper was a devoted family
man with four daughters, and he usually seemed to have
time for people like me. I once asked him how he managed it all. He replied, "You learn to manage the church's
ministries and dreams very well, or the work will kill
you." This book unpacks the ways that Christian leaders
manage their churches, institutions, movements, and
dreams "very well."

You may have a problem with the management perspective, however. Perhaps six out of ten church leaders
who have read this far will NOT take the management
challenge seriously enough to change the way they do
anything. Many pastors, and other church professionals,
"*need* to be needed," and the more people who need
them, the more needed they feel. Moreover, many pastors and church workers *like* to be everybody's chaplain;
they care for all their members, and they contact, counsel, and pray with people at the local barbershop, fire
station, hospital, nursing home, and Moose lodge.

In either pattern, such church professionals do not
want to get ministry done through other people; they
want, or need, to do it all themselves. They may rational-
ize what they need or like by suggesting that their theological education, or their ordination, uniquely qualifies
them to represent the Christian faith and care for people.

At an intellectual level, this orientation so violently contrasts with the early church's character as a lay movement, with the later Protestant doctrine of the Priesthood of All Believers, and with the lay ministry behind the great growth of the church wherever it is occurring today that it is easily refuted. But, I have discovered, a good refutation makes no enduring difference. Therapy might, but the lives of "chaplains" are driven much more by emotion-based needs and desires than by informed intellectual conviction.

Chapter Two: A Defense of Management to Its "Spiritual Despisers"

A couple of centuries ago, Friedrich Schleiermacher defended and commended Christianity to the world's "Cultured Despisers," that is, Europe's educated elite. Today, however, we need to defend and commend some of the secular world's bodies of knowledge to some of their "Spiritual Despisers" within the church. This book commends "management" to Christian leaders who want their churches to reach pre-Christian people and experience healthy growth. The first chapter introduced management as the informed art of getting things done through other people. It ended with an admission that many church leaders who need or prefer to do all the ministry themselves will, understandably, bypass the lore of management. However, I meet two negative reactions to the idea of church management that are more substantial, whose devotees are sometimes persuaded by an academic response.

First, some church leaders resist insights from the literatures of leadership, management, and organization effectiveness because, they say, "The church is different. The church isn't an organization, it is an organism—the Body of Christ. Christ is its head, he is the leader, and we are called to run the church on spiritual principles, not the principles of Madison Avenue and the corporate world."

This "spiritual" perspective on the church does contain a crucial perspective on this matter. The church is, or should be, different from McDonald's, Sears, Rotary, GM, IBM, MIT, and P&G. Ignoring the fact that each of those seven organizations is very different from the other six, five things (at least) do make the church a different kind of organization: (1) The church has a distinct source. Christ built it, on the rock of faith in him as Messiah and risen Lord, to be the New Israel, the Body of Christ, and the extension of his incarnation. (2) From the ancient apostles, the church has a distinct message—the gospel. That is why Leander Keck, former dean of Yale Divinity School, coaches church leaders to "spend your life offering the gospel to the world, because it is the only thing we have to offer the world that it doesn't already have."[1] (3) The church has a distinct purpose—to reach the peoples of the earth, to help them become reconciled to God, liberated from their sins, restored to God's purpose, and deployed in God's wider mission seeking health, peace, justice, and salvation for all people and (some would add) all creation. (4) Through such sources as the Ten Commandments, the Sermon on the Mount, and the Great Commandment to love God and neighbor, the church is given the ethic that should limit, shape, and focus how Christians do Kingdom business. (5) As "no one can say 'Jesus is Lord' except by the Holy Spirit" (1 Cor. 12:3), not much else that is supremely important in our total mission is likely to succeed without Third Person power behind, attending, and blessing our efforts.

Though the church is a different kind of organization, however, it is still an organization. In common with other organizations, the church is an interdependent aggregation of people with some shared history, identity, and culture, who pull together in coordinated activities to achieve the organization's objectives. Granting its distinctive source, message, mission, ethic, and reliance, churches nevertheless have much in common with other organizations, particularly other voluntary organizations. When churches achieve their objectives, many of the reasons are the same as when other kinds of organizations achieve their objectives. If it helps to know, much of the best literature on leadership and management is written by devoted Christians, such as Peter Drucker and Ken Blanchard. Nevertheless, there is no "Christian" body of management theory any more than there is a "Christian" grammar or a "Christian" arithmetic or a "Christian" chemistry or a "Christian" way to train for the decathlon. Presumably, Christians who are effective in the world (while no longer of it) will connect subjects and predicates or calculate the square root of a number or measure and mix a solution or prepare for a shot put competition more or less like anyone else.

Occasionally, I meet church leaders who deny all of this. I have concluded, reluctantly, that they may be "heretics"—harboring a docetic ecclesiology! That glib charge warrants an explanation. In the first centuries of Christianity, some Christians were influenced by a Greek philosophy called Gnosticism. Gnostics believed that matter, and particularly the human body, is evil. Gnostic Christians believed, therefore, that in the Incarnation God did not really take on human flesh, and Christ could not possibly have suffered on the cross; he only appeared to be human, and he only appeared to suffer, like an actor playing a role in a salvation drama. FitzSimon Allison explains their view and their label:

> The Docetists found it incomprehensible that Jesus could have actually suffered. They answered the essential questions about him by insisting that he only *appeared* to suffer, to weep, to thirst, to hunger, to sweat in agony, and to die, and that his

incarnate human state was so spiritual that he only appeared to be human. (Docetism is derived from the word *dokein*, which means "to seem, to appear.")[2]

The Council of Nicaea branded this view a serious heresy and affirmed that Jesus Christ was indeed "begotten, not made man," "was crucified," "suffered death and was buried." The Council insisted that Jesus took on our full humanity because, in the words of ancient theologians, "What he did not assume, he could not save," and, "He became as we are, that we might become like him."

Docetism is still with us, in several forms, but "docetic ecclesiology" may be a new form. As the old Docetism claimed that Jesus' body was not a real human body, though it appeared to be, docetic ecclesiology maintains that the church, the Body of Christ, is not a real human organization, though it appears to be. An orthodox doctrine of the church, however, would affirm the church's full humanity. As Jesus' body was a real human body— as any physician checking for a pulse or a blood pressure reading could have affirmed—so the Body of Christ is a real human organization, reflecting many of the same dynamics and managed by many of the same principles we find in other organizations. The church, because of its distinct source, message, mission, ethic, and reliance, is a different kind of organization than Honda or Harvard, but an organization nevertheless. The most effective Christian leaders will be informed both by what we know about organizations and by what we know about churches.[3]

The second substantial negative reaction surfaces from church leaders who claim (in a trendy distinction) "I am not a manager, I am a *leader!*" (Their tone usually suggests that some tasks are "beneath" them.) Some writers, such as Warren Bennis, do indeed distinguish between leadership and management. In *Leaders: Strategies for Taking Charge*, a splendid book based on research that essentially redefined what we think we know about leadership, Bennis addressed a widespread problem in the business world: "The problem with many organizations, and especially the ones that are failing, is that they tend to be overmanaged and under-led."[4] How does Bennis nuance this distinction? Leading, he observes, has more to do with projecting the organization's vision, purpose, and course and with influencing and mobilizing the people in pursuit of that vision. Managing has more to do with taking responsibility for the organization and seeing that the organization's goals are accomplished.[5] With some hyperbole, Bennis remarks that "managers are people who do things right and leaders are people who do the right thing." Leaders are concerned with "effectiveness," managers with "efficiency."[6] The distinction is important, but it is not new; only the words have changed. Thirty years ago, several writers claimed that "administrators do things right and managers do the right thing." This semantic shift, involving three terms— leader, manager, and administrator—calls for a moment of analysis.

In 1990, John Kotter published an influential *Harvard Business Review* article entitled "What Leaders Really Do," in which he argued that "management is about coping with complexity," while "Leadership is about coping with change." [7] Transparently, as organizations become more complex and as environments become more competitive and volatile, organizations need both leadership and management to be effective. More specifically, in Kotter's thought, leadership focuses on setting the organization's overall direction and aligning and motivating people; management focuses on planning and budgeting, organizing and staffing, controlling and problem solving. While some people's aptitudes make them good managers but not good leaders, and others make good leaders but not good managers, the ideal is to develop leader-managers.

More recently, Ken Blanchard confesses to being less and less interested in arguments about the difference between leading and managing, and he advocates another reason for the leader-manager. While Blanchard affirms the useful distinction between Direction and Implementation, he suggests that, in many organizations

> the people who have created the vision and direction of the organization—the top managers—don't roll up their sleeves and get involved in implementation. It always seems to be left to others in the organization. As a result, a lot of organizations are running with their brakes on. If you have ever driven a car with the brakes on, you know what happens when you finally release them. The car surges forward with tremendous energy. I think that will happen when we get the behavior or implementation of a vision lined up with that vision.[8]

My experience in church organizations persuades me that all three terms, and another—leader, manager, administrator, and executive—are useful in understanding how churches, and church organizations, are guided and pulled in ways that help achieve their missions. I propose the following distinctions: Leadership is the most important role of the three. A *leader* communicates the church's vision, purpose, and direction and mobilizes people's energy in support of it. A *manager* deploys people (and resources), through specific roles, jobs, and tasks, to achieve the mission's purpose and sees to it that the organization permits and helps the people to succeed. An *administrator* facilitates the workflow of the organization and attends to its efficiency. The obsession of the first role is direction, the second is effectiveness, the third is efficiency.

All three roles—leader, manager, and administrator— are executive roles, and most any organization needs all three. (Some people, in my seminars, have reluctantly agreed that leaders and managers are needed, but they are undecided whether administrators are "a necessary evil" or "the root of all evil"! But a church organization informed by a doctrine of stewardship, like a theological seminary, really does need a comptroller, a personnel administrator, an admissions officer, and a registrar, to run a tight, legal, efficient, faithful ship.)

Moreover, every effective executive exercises all three roles in some proportion, as needed. For instance, the President of the United States obviously plays a leadership role and that is the most essential role, but he also manages the cabinet and the White House staff, and he also attends to some administrative tasks to assure that the work is done with precision and excellence. Likewise, many people in an essentially administrative role, like the seminary's comptroller or registrar, manage a staff and, in their areas at least, exercise leadership for the seminary.

This perspective permits us to reflect, for church organizations, upon Bennis's observation that too many organizations are "overmanaged and underled." I have indeed observed that pathology in some churches and church organizations, but I have observed two other pathologies at least as often.

First, some church organizations, like some church-related colleges, are overadministered, undermanaged, and underled! The people attend innumerable meetings and fill out an endless stream of reports, but no one reminds them of the purpose the organization serves, and no one makes sure they have what they need to do their jobs.

Second, many church organizations are overled and undermanaged! While, as Bennis observes, many secular organizations have managers who cannot lead, many churches and church organizations have leaders who cannot manage! Consider the most blatant widespread example: the thousands of preachers who inspire their people to "go out and change the world." Once the service is over, the people are never asked to do anything specific! In this pathology's many forms, the pastor casts the vision and calls the people to mission, and the people are aroused and energized, but the follow-through is ineffective (or nonexistent), the mission is not achieved, and the people become disillusioned. This problem is seldom seen in secular organizations; so this is another way in which many church organizations are different from their more secular counterparts. The church attracts a disproportionate number of people who can lead, but cannot (yet) manage. This is a long-standing problem in the Judeo-Christian tradition. Indeed, this was the very problem that hounded Moses and the Israelites until Jethro stepped in.

Chapter Three:
Standing on the Shoulders of Moses

The life of Moses provides a classic study in the development of a supremely significant leader, and manager. The context in which Moses arose as a leader, the enslavement of his people in Egypt, reflects the adage that great leaders often emerge in times of great need. The story reports that Moses, as an infant, was rescued for God's eventual purpose from the bulrushes and adopted into Pharaoh's household. The God of Abraham was preparing Moses for his ultimate purpose by having him raised with the educational advantages and the political insight that he would gain from life in Pharaoh's household. Moses stepped into his "first career," and performed effectively in a management role for Pharoah's government. Following that preparation, God, through the burning bush experience, entrusted Moses with the clear vision of his people set free from bondage and placed in a Promised Land, and the Voice commissioned Moses to lead that cause. Moses hid his face from God's presence, a Hebrew cultural expression telling us that Moses knew he was unworthy of God's confidence and commission.

The story, bathed in realism, emphasizes that Moses'

"second career" as a leader for the Jewish people was no "instant winner." When, to Pharaoh, Moses declared "Thus says the LORD, the God of Israel, 'Let my people go' " (Exod. 5:1). Pharaoh laughed and increased the people's workload; the slaves were now compelled to make more bricks, with no additional allotment of straw for making the bricks. When Moses spoke to the people, to share their God's vision of freedom and a Promised Land, the text tells us in Exodus 6:9 "They would not listen to Moses, because of their broken spirit and their cruel slavery." Additional attempts to move Pharaoh were unproductive. Only a series of calamities—plagues of frogs, gnats, and locusts, and the death of Egypt's first-born male babies—convinced Pharaoh to let the people go. Soon after they set off, Pharaoh changed his mind and sent his soldiers in pursuit of the Jews. The people made it across the Red Sea because the waters parted for them and then closed upon the pursuing army. The story then dramatizes the giddy euphoria that people experience following a milestone victory against great odds. Miriam, sister of Moses, leads the people in singing

> Sing to the LORD, for he has
> triumphed gloriously;
> horse and rider he has thrown
> into the sea. (Exod. 15:21)

Then, Moses discovered a reality that usually attaches to the leadership experience, a reality that blindsides most new leaders. The higher up you go in an organization, the more people there are who appraise your performance! All of the people were appraising Moses' performance. As the people, within hours of their liberation, began experiencing hunger, the text (Exod. 16:2, RSV) tells us that "the people of Israel murmured against Moses." When they became thirsty, "the people found fault with Moses" (Exod. 17:2, RSV).

Moses responded to the flood of criticism like a typical pastor. He devoted himself, personally, to covering all of their needs and meeting all of their demands and expectations. Exodus 18:13 gives us this graphic description: "The people stood about Moses from morning till evening" (RSV). What was Moses doing during those long days? He was teaching them what he knew about their God; he was giving spiritual direction regarding God's law and will; and, case by case, he was settling and adjudicating disputes among the people—conflict resolution! Notice this indispensable lesson in Moses' management education: Moses was doing it all, morning, afternoon, and evening, seven days a week, and still the people were not satisfied!

At this point, Moses' father-in-law, Jethro, changed roles and became the first known Organization Consultant. He gained Moses' attention with these unforgettable words: "What you are doing is not good." Moses was undoubtedly confused. Good was the only thing he was doing! He had no time for anything else! He was doing good around the clock! Yet Jethro said, "What you are doing is not good." I have not confirmed this translation from the original Hebrew, because the only Hebrew words I remember are "Elohim" and "Taj Mahal." But the half dozen English translations I checked all say, and mean, the same thing to Moses (and to us): Spending your life, overtime, doing good is not good. Jethro explains *why* this is "not good." Moses would only wear himself out. Moses could not do it all anyway. Moses and the people would never reach the Promised Land this way.

Jethro then recommended a way of organizing and managing the work of the people of God that would enable the community, including Moses, to be healthy and to fulfill their vision. Moses was to organize the people by tens, fifties, one hundreds, and one thousands. Moses

31

would choose and develop leaders for each of those levels. Moses responded rapidly. He became a teacher, and taught all of the people, at one time, what had been revealed to him of the law and will of their God. Furthermore, Moses became a manager, who would get the work of God done primarily through other people. Other leaders, beginning at the level of tens, would do spiritual direction and conflict resolution. Some cases would be referred, or appealed, upward. Moses would act only on the cases too difficult for four preceding leaders. Moses would have a life and a marriage and time to reflect and pray and smell the roses once again.

Moses, after the initial setbacks in Egypt, proved to be a great leader who could sell the vision, energize the people, and get them moving. Now Moses became the manager who could achieve the movement's objectives through other people. There is one point in the story that is easy to misinterpret. You could walk away with the idea that Moses became an instant manager, that Jethro told him it was necessary, and Moses simply did it. There is no evidence of a management education, or even further coaching, following Jethro's intervention. I have had students who assumed that if you become convinced you need to do it, you can simply do it—no management education required.

Actually, the reason Moses could implement Jethro's management model so readily was because he was already intimately familiar with the principles. God had arranged for Moses to be raised in Pharaoh's household, that Moses might observe firsthand how the organizational world works. Moses would have observed that Pharaoh did not even try to do everything himself. Most of what it took to run an empire was delegated. In his first career, Moses had played an upper-middle-management role in the Egyptian government. Now, the senior leadership role with the people of God became his second career. However, like many second-career people in ministry leadership, Moses had not made the connection. He was oblivious to the possibility that what he had learned before was useful now, that God was preparing him in his upbringing and his first job for his eventual calling. After Jethro made the connection for him, Moses began managing effectively very quickly because he was already schooled in the process; he already knew how to manage! Notice, when Moses included the management process within his leadership of the people of God, he did not become any less of a leader than before; he became a more effective leader.

So the biblical tradition has been aware of the relevance of the management challenge since twelve hundred years before Christ. Christian leaders, today, are discovering that effective management is a prerequisite to, and a prominent cause of, growing healthy churches. Of course, management skill by itself never made any church a growing redemptive power. Factors such as the leadership's biblical rootage, openness to the Holy Spirit, and love for people are much more important. But most churches will not do the will of God and fulfill their destiny unless the leaders, like Moses, get their act together and achieve most of the ministry and mission through many other people. Thousands of churches need more effective management of their ministries.

Fortunately, the practice of effective management can be learned. In the long-standing dispute over whether leaders are born or made, we now know that aptitude is an undoubted factor, but leaders who can manage are mostly shaped, like Moses, by their education, life experience, and driving purpose.

Chapter Four: The Management Perspective: Roots, Questions, Tasks

Management, as a discipline informing the art or practice of managing an organization of people, is essentially a field conceived and developed in the second half of the twentieth century. Its contemporary development is usually dated from the publication of Peter Drucker's *Practice of Management* (1954). The discipline's continued development is informed today by the research in university schools of management like Stanford, Harvard, Pennsylvania, Northwestern, and Chicago and, increasingly, in schools of education and many other institutions. Such research does not confine its interest to "business"; the discipline also informs the management of educational institutions, government and public institutions, churches and other nonprofit organizations, and even community development and movements. In the early 1980s, Tom Peters and Bob Waterman's *In Search of Excellence* led a global interest in managing effective organizations of all kinds. The American Management Association (AMA), with headquarters in New York City, has schooled more developing managers and leaders than any other institution.

The 1970s, 1980s, and 1990s witnessed a welcome maturity in the literature of the management revolution. Once, in a more headstrong adolescent phase of the revolution, management knowledge was regarded as a panacea. Its champions believed that "he who can manage can manage anything," that one simply "must know how to act like a manager in any situation calling for management, for leadership."[1] While there is much truth in this earlier confidence—that management skills are generic and therefore infinitely adaptable to all kinds of organizations, we now know that, in today's more complex and more rapidly changing world, one cannot effectively manage a business without knowing the specific business. For instance, when Stephen Jobs brought John Scully from Pepsi Cola to become president of Apple Computer Company, Scully discovered the need to learn a whole lot about computers, the computer industry, computer markets, software companies, and so forth, before he could manage Apple effectively. A hypothetical instance makes the same point: if General Patton had retired and gone into the ministry and become senior pastor of First Church, he would have learned the differences between military and religious organizations, and between an army's main business and a church's main business, and between military and church people, or he would have failed. To manage a faithful, growing, effective church, one must know the church's scriptures, history, traditions, culture, ethic, liturgies, and mission, and one must also know the adaptable principles of effective management.

For the most part, however, the church at every level has not shared in the twentieth century's "management revolution." Though its Kingdom purposes are more important than the purposes of any other organization, the church has not taken the effective pursuit of its mission with the radical seriousness in which, say, IBM, McDonald's, Disney, Stanford, or the New York Yankees pursue their distinctive perennial missions. Most of our laypeople now work in organizations that are far better led and managed than their church. When some people compare the great purposes of the church's world mission—to feed and nurture the hungry, to advance peace and justice, and to communicate the gospel and make disciples among all peoples—with the ineffective ways we pursue those purposes, they understandably wonder whether we really believe in Christ's mission and whether we really intend to achieve great things. Indeed, shouldn't the organization with the greatest mission pursue that mission through the best possible methods?

The purpose of this book is to immerse church leaders in a crash course in the essential principles for managing any organization—from a family to a corporation. What is stressed in this chapter are the fundamental questions that any effective manager must ask, and the (matching) generic tasks that any effective manager must perform. One source, with some adaptation, is the four week Management Course of the American Management Association,[2] which has more graduates than any other management curriculum in the world. The course's core principles are published in *Formula for Success: A Core Concept of Management* by Lawrence A. Appley, who served as the AMA president for twenty years.[3]

Appley assures us, in the first paragraph of the preface, that "even religion relies upon good management in order to be effective in human life."[4] He explains that "the core concept of management is this: Management is getting things done through other people. Management, therefore, becomes any activity which involves leading any group of people toward the attainment of common objectives in any walk of life."[5]

Appley advocated management as the key to "purposeful action," the "means for making things happen rather than letting them happen."[6] The AMA believes they have demonstrated that effective managers "can be trained . . . for leadership in the church, the government, the school, the labor union, in business, in industry, and in any other segment of human endeavor."[7]

The heart of the AMA Management Course resides in (a) eight questions that all effective managers ask, and in (b) ten tasks that are involved in the essential process of management. The eight questions and ten tasks can be correlated and outlined as follows:

Questions Managers Ask	The Tasks of Management
1. Where is the organization now?	1. Situation Analysis (or Inventory)
2. Where do we want the organization to go?	2. Planning
3. What people do we need to get there?	3. Organizing Human Resources
4. What do the people need to get there?	4. Organizing Physical Resources
5. How well should our people work?	5. Standards of Performance
6. How well are our people working?	6. Appraisal of Performance
7. How can we help people do better?	7. Development 8. Controls
8. How will we reward our people?	9. Incentives 10. Rewards

The overall process of managing an organization's achievement can be readily understood in terms of a familiar family challenge—taking a vacation trip by car. You begin (situation analysis) consulting your map by pinpointing your present location; you assess the health of the car, the heat of the day, and the hostility level of the family, and you decide to go for it. You identify your destination and *plan* the trip, including the route, the schedule, and who will drive while the other is managing the escalating sibling rivalry present in a minivan carrying (human resources) two adults and three kids, as well as a standard poodle and fifty toys for two long driving days. You reserve a motel room for the night you will be en route; and you confirm your possession of the cash and credit cards to cover meals, gas, entertainment, emergencies, and surprises (physical resources). You determine you must wear seatbelts, average forty miles per hour, stick to the itinerary, and avoid collisions (standards of performance), and periodically you *appraise* your performance by these standards. Along the way, you coach your oldest kid in map interpretation (development), and you stop the car to control a pillow fight before the youngest kid is smothered. By afternoon of the second day you promise Baskin Robbins pit stops and a major league baseball game (incentives and rewards) if only you arrive at Grandma's with your sanity intact.

Chapter Five:
Situation Analysis for the Local Church

The effective leadership and management of churches begins with two of the most essential questions for determining any organization's future: "Where are we now?" and "Where do we want to go?" This chapter addresses the first question, and the next chapter addresses the second, but in "real life" they are best considered together. The importance of planning for churches is reflected in Robert Schuller's observation that "If you fail to plan, you plan to fail!"

By that standard, over 80 percent of all the churches of North America "plan to fail." More than 80 percent of our churches do not have plans for impacting their community and for serving and reaching pre-Christian people, or any informed plan for their future. Without a strategic plan for, say, the next five years that the people own and are implementing, a church is not likely to achieve very much. It will be a victim of the social, economic, and demographic trends of the surrounding community, but will not be one of the forces impacting and shaping the future of the community.

Planning necessarily begins with a situation analysis, such as gathering and organizing the relevant facts and data which will inform the church's planning for its future. Notice: Planning can be no better then the data that the planning builds upon; as computer buffs say, "Garbage in, garbage out!" Bob Waterman quotes A. E. Housman as declaring that "the house of delusion is cheap to build but drafty to live in."[1] In underscoring the importance of "the facts," Waterman refers to Lee Iacocca's experience of taking the helm of a (then) declining Chrysler Corporation, as reported in his auto-biography:

> "Gradually I was finding that Chrysler had no overall system of financial controls . . . even the most rudimentary [financial] questions were impossible for them to answer. But never mind the answers; these guys didn't even know the questions!" Iacocca recalls how he asked in vain for a list of Chrysler plants ranked by their rate of return on investment. "I couldn't find out *anything*. This was probably the greatest jolt I've ever had in my business career."[2]

Waterman concludes that "most successful turn-arounds, it seems, begin with a search for the friendly facts."

Churches are very different kinds of organizations than automobile corporations, of course, so the type of data most needed to inform church planning for turn-around, growth, and renewed effectiveness will be different. In my experience, an informed approach to analyzing a church's current situation and opportunity involves discovering and organizing five distinct kinds of data:

A. Identify the social, economic, religious, and demographic facts, trends, and projections in the wider community in which the church serves and intends to reach some people and carve out a future.

In the U.S., the congregation's best single source for quickly, and inexpensively, accessing this data is the parachurch organization PERCEPT. In the computer and Internet age, PERCEPT can access the U.S. Census and many other population data bases, and find out who lives within your church's ministry area; indeed, the organization can help you define, or redefine, your ministry area if that is necessary. PERCEPT can then shape much of the intelligence you need for planning in astonishingly useful ways. In regard to "PERCEPT's 50 U.S. Lifestyle Segments," the group can tell you how many "Rising Potential Professionals," or how many "Established Empty Nesters," or how many "New Beginning Urbanites," or how many "Struggling Hispanic Households" there are in your target ministry area. They can even estimate, for each population, the kind of issues and needs the people struggle with, and the kind of church, ministries, programs, and worship services they would most likely respond to. (You can contact PERCEPT by calling 1-800-442-6277.)

You can gain additional demographic information by networking with the local leaders who already possess, work with, and plan by it—such as a school system superintendent, a city planner, or the relevant marketing person for McDonald's or Sears. You may have to dig for some of the data, like in the most recent Census data for your community available in the local library (or on the Internet), but it is worth digging for, and there is usually someone in the church with digging experience or an eagerness to learn. If several churches in your ministry area are already growing, someone will need to observe and interview leaders, new converts, and so forth to determine the causes of church growth already occurring in that population setting.

You should interview a sampling of, say, two hundred unchurched people in your community. You cannot reach people whom you do not understand, and there is no shortcut to interviewing enough people to understand some of the perceptions, attitudes, needs, and feelings of the population they represent. Before the founding members of Willow Creek Community Church led their first service in 1975, they interviewed hundreds of unchurched people. They asked, "Do you regularly attend a local church?" If the people responded "No," Creekers asked "Would you be willing to tell me why you don't?"[3] Their insights from the interviews influenced the way they did church to reach the very population in which they did the interviews. In *How to Reach Secular People*, I summarized their most important discoveries as follows.

> Willow Creek's approach is based on their research of the unchurched populations of metropolitan Chicago, and on the resulting profile of "Unchurched Harry." Their research told them that if Harry decides to visit a church he wants: (1) anonymity: he wants to be left alone to look it over, he doesn't want to say anything, or sign anything, or "be recognized." (2) Harry wants things to happen at an introductory level—so he can understand. (3) He wants relevance. It has to make a difference in his life situation, or he will conclude that: "Christianity doesn't relate to my life," so Hybels especially wants his "messages" (not "sermons") to have "high user-take-home-value." (4) Harry's enculturation in the professional world of Chicago primes him to expect "excellence" from a church service he is willing to take seriously; if it is "bush league" he will write it off. (5) Harry wants time to decide—with respect for his questions, without pressure to make up his mind.

B. Learn what you can about the "culture" of each population you are called to serve. "Culture" is variously defined as "the silent language" or "the software of the mind" or the "lens" through which a people perceives reality or the "learned, shared, and integrated pattern of customs, attitudes, beliefs, and values characteristic of a society." In the fields of cultural anthropology, missiology, and intercultural communication, we have identified about fourteen "macro-cultures" on earth, about thirty thousand "cultures," and a great many more "subcultures," "microcultures," and "countercultures," and we have learned that, at least in Western societies, each generation seems to develop its own "generational culture" within the wider culture.

While a course in cultural anthropology is outside the scope of this book, this much should alert you to the fact that your church's ministry area is probably composed of a number of people groups, each with its own distinct cultural orientation. The challenge facing your leaders is to understand the cultural "soil" in which you are called to plant the seed of God's Word. This challenge is imposing, and you have some limitations: You may never understand Mexican-Americans, Generation Xers, or the Culture of Addiction as well as an insider. The realistic challenge is to understand them enough, to adapt to them enough, to engage their most receptive bi-cultural members, train them for ministry, and support their movement to their people. If you prayerfully search for them, you will find a few of "them" who are open to the gospel, who understand your culture well enough to meet you halfway, and who understand their culture enough, and have influence enough, to serve as bridges and leaders of a new Christian movement.

Somewhat at the surface level (using the acronym SLAM), you will discover what you can about the Style, the Language, the Aesthetics, and the Music that are indigenous to their culture. At a deeper level, you will discover what you can about the characteristic beliefs and values of their culture.

Intercultural communication scholar John Condon has identified many categories, with two or three options in each category, for helping us to "exegete" someone else's culture. [4] For example, in their source of identity are they individualists or people with a group identity, or collectivists? Do they most value youth, middle age, or old age? Are they democratic or authoritarian? Informal or formal?

What is their view of human nature? Do they believe that humans are rational, intuitive, or irrational? Are humans good, evil, or some mixture? Is human life mostly happiness, sadness, or some mixture? Are humans supposed to dominate nature, live in harmony with nature, or be dominated by nature? Should people live oriented toward the past, the present, or the future? Should human life's goals be material, intellectual, or spiritual? Can human beings change, or is personality fixed?

What are their assumptions about the world and the wider cosmos? Is it mechanistic, spiritual, or organic? Is it comprehensible, incomprehensible, or some combination of "faith and reason"? Is it friendly, impersonal, or hostile?

David Burnett, a British anthropologist, has contributed a significant set of ten questions to guide us in our observations and interviews:[5]

1. What beliefs are strongly held?

2. How do parents teach children to behave?

3. What do people regard as major offenses (sins)?

4. What do people do in crises?

5. What rituals do people perform?

6. Who are the trendsetters?

7. What are the greatest fears that people have?

8. What are considered to be words of wisdom?

9. What is expressed in the art forms of the people?

10. What aspects of the culture are most resistant to change?

Over the years of studying about, observing, and interviewing in many North American and European cultures, I have developed an additional list that somewhat overlaps with Burnett's:

1. What are their distinctive behaviors, habits, and pastimes? What beliefs, attitudes, or values might these reflect?

2. What appear to be their goals in life? What drives them?

3. Who/what types are their heroes, heroines, and role models? What does this tell us about them?

4. What are the pivotal defining events in their conscious history?

5. What are their conscious struggles, problems, and felt needs?

6. What are their predominant beliefs and values?

7. What kind(s) of music do they really like?

8. What are the themes of their music, movies, stories, legends, and so on?

9. How do they perceive the world? History? The future?

10. What are their taboos and hang-ups? What turns them off?

45

11. What is their "image" of God? Jesus Christ? The church? Christianity? The Bible?

12. What do they assume Christianity is basically about? Stands for? Offers? Requires in response?

13. What can we learn from those who have become Christians about approaches to effectively reach others like them?

14. What can members of the target population teach us about reaching them?

C. Identify your church's "type" within its wider community. The most useful single way to type your church is probably not in terms of its size, or denominational tradition or the color of brick, so much as by three other factors: (a) its location, (b) the people it presently reaches and serves, and (c) their understanding of their community within the total community. Of those three factors, the third is the most important. Essentially, most people in American cities today seem to display one of four "neighboring patterns."

1. Some people, "cosmopolitans," claim and experience the whole city as their community.

2. Some people, even in the automobile age, still do their "neighboring" within their residential neighborhood.

3. Some people neighbor within a larger region of the city.

4. Some people relate to a widespread "homogeneous" network of persons with whom they

share the same language, culture, subculture, background, handicap, or interest.

Ezra Earl Jones was the first to observe that, essentially, these four populations are served, respectively, by the "Downtown First Church," the "Neighborhood Church," the "Regional Church," and the "Special Purpose Church."[6] In *To Spread the Power: Church Growth in the Wesleyan Spirit*, I unpacked this typology for church growth planning, now modified for this book:[7]

1. The *Downtown First Church* was the first church of its denomination in the city. Its founding generation included many of the city's pioneers and founding leaders. Typically, first church "planted" most of the other churches of that denomination throughout the city.

Located downtown, first church has the strategic advantage of being located on "neutral turf." In the people's social perceptions in most cities, downtown "belongs" to everyone; when someone visits first church they do not feel they are trespassing on someone else's turf. This helps first church attract a more heterogeneous congregation than any other type of church.

Furthermore, first church attracts many of the cosmopolitans who think of the whole city as their community. Indeed, the cosmopolitans across the city are first church's most obvious "market." First church can engage cosmopolitans much more effectively than the other three types of churches. Some church types, particularly the Neighborhood Church, will not engage many cosmopolitans at all.

2. The *Neighborhood Church* is located in, and largely of, a residential neighborhood of a city or suburb. Sometimes it carries the neighborhood's name, as in

Edgewood Presbyterian Church. Sometimes it is located adjacent to the neighborhood school.

The neighborhood church's future is strongly tied to the neighborhood's future. Most of the people it reaches live in the neighborhood, or in an adjacent neighborhood. It especially reaches the people who still neighbor with their neighbors. In many neighborhood churches, the church's members used to live in the neighborhood, but moved out (and "up"), and they continue to drive in for worship at the old neighborhood church. Their children will not return, however, when they reach adulthood. The ex-residents of the neighborhood who still return are less likely to accept leadership roles, while those who do are often insensitive to the community's changes and opportunities, and may be emotionally committed to keeping the church "the way it has always been."

3. The *Regional Church* is a visible church, located on the major traffic artery (or at the intersection of two main traffic arteries) in an identifiable region of the city. It may carry the region's popular name, as in Southland Christian Church or West End United Methodist Church. It attracts people from "this side of town," especially people who think of that section of the city as their community. The regional church frequently grows to great institutional strength and strongly supports the wider mission of the denomination.

4. The *Special Purpose Church* exists (get this!) for some special purpose. Compared to the first three types, location has less to do with this church's effectiveness. It engages people of a particular language, background, handicap, or cause. So, for instance, Akron, Ohio, has Korean churches, culturally Appalachian churches, deaf churches, recovery churches, and peace churches, among many others.

Ezra Earl Jones's church typology includes two other types of churches that dot the American landscape beyond the cities:

5. The *Town Church* is located at the commercial core of a town with a metropolitan area population of between five hundred and twenty thousand. It may be, particularly in smaller towns, the only church of its denomination. Similar in many ways to the downtown church, it is located in "everybody's territory" and can therefore attract people from a wide ministry area.

6. An *Open Country* church is located on a rural highway, or on some secondary road in open country. It serves the people who live in a sparsely settled rural area, or those who have moved to town and return to worship— but whose children will not return when they grow up.[8]

When a church's leaders understand their church's "type" within this typology, this perspective helps shape the questions they ask, the opportunities they perceive, and the strategies for ministry they develop.

For instance, a neighborhood church is typically impacted by demographic changes in its neighborhood. The neighborhood, within several years, may change from upper middle class to lower middle class, from Anglo to African American, from educated African Americans to less educated African Americans, from Hispanic to Haitian, and so forth. An urban neighborhood may substantially change three or four times within a generation.

Some neighborhood churches succeed in adapting to the demographic trends, while other churches do not (and they become "ex-neighborhood churches"). Ezra Earl Jones observes that one crucial variable resides in the early perceptions of the church's leaders. If they perceive the change as a problem or as an old community dying, the church probably will not make it; but if they perceive the change as an opportunity or as a new community being born and yet to take shape, the church will probably survive and may even thrive. I have observed that a second crucial variable centers in the way the leaders assimilate the church's first members from the new population. If some members of the target population are expeditiously prepared and placed in visible leadership roles, then the new people will feel that the church is "our church too." (There are never many people standing in line to become permanent guests in someone else's church!)

Again, a growing number of leaders in open country churches are perceiving a larger harvest than their predecessors. They have decided that the automobile is probably here to stay, and the average family will probably continue to have one or more cars. They have reasoned, therefore, that they should not be constrained by the "parish" mentality of their predecessors whose imagination reached no farther than the radius in which people could walk to church. They now define every unchurched person within, say, twenty minutes driving time as within "our mission field." Furthermore, they see opportunities as early retirees move to the countryside, and as others build homes in the country and commute to work in the city on the new interstate highway.

The Jones typology also helps churches of each type understand, and live with, their limitations. The typology helps downtown first church people understand why they cannot reach many of the urban neighborhood people who live in proximity to the church, and why the neighborhood storefront church down the street can reach them. It helps the neighborhood church understand why some people who live in the neighborhood bypass their church to go to the regional or downtown church. It helps the English-speaking regional church understand why the Koreans they invite would rather go to the Korean-language church in another part of the city.

The Jones typology also provides perspective for a denomination's new church planting strategy. In many cities today, there are probably too many neighborhood churches trying to serve a declining market of people who still neighbor with their neighbors. However, I know of no city where there are enough regional churches or enough special purpose churches.

D. Track your church's "membership strength" trends for the past decade, and project those trends for the next decade. In the Church Growth movement, we typically work with three indicators of membership strength that are usually available in church and denominational records: (a) membership at the end of each reporting year, (b) average worship attendance per year, and (c) average Sunday school attendance per year. It is almost always possible to excavate those three data for each of the last ten years and graph them to dramatize the trends in membership strength, and then to project the trends ten years into the future—to show what the church's membership strength will be in a decade if present trends, policies, priorities, programs, staffing, and so on, merely continue. With that projection in view, it is natural for the leadership group to ask, "Is that where we want to be ten years from now?" If not, they are motivated to project where they do want to go, and then develop and implement plans to achieve the desired strength.[9]

I strongly recommend the use of additional data for estimating the church's membership strength. They are data not normally collected for reporting to the denomination, but a serious church could begin collecting these data this year for the sake of its future planning and effectiveness. You will recall the three data mentioned above:

1. Church membership at the end of each year

2. Average worship attendance for each year

3. Average Sunday School Attendance for each year

Some strategic churches have found it useful to collect data, and discern membership strength trends, in some areas of church life that more closely reflect their essential mission and priorities, such as:

4. People received, each year, as new Christians from the world (Conversion Growth)

5. Number of people, each year, regularly involved in any lay ministry to people

6. Average attendance, each year, in small groups where people are in ministry to each other or have some external ministry

7. The number, each year, of regular pledged giving units to the church's budget

8. The percentage, each year, of the church's budget devoted to mission beyond the church and local community

9. The number of people, each year, involved in the church's scheduled prayer ministries

10. The number of people, each year, regularly studying the scriptures with other people

11. The number of people, each year, involved in short-term cross-cultural mission experiences

12. The number of missionaries supported by the church who are engaged in apostolic ministry to some pre-Christian population.

I have studied churches using each of these indicators of membership strength, though I have observed no church using them all, nor would I necessarily recommend that! It does demonstrate that a more comprehensive approach to membership strength analysis is more possible than we have usually featured in church growth literature. Moreover, it shows that no church's data for self-analysis should be limited to the data that the denomination expects.

But is it desirable to collect "more statistics"? You do not, of course, want to get bogged down in "the paralysis of analysis." But some of the students of social movements tell us that perhaps the most important variable determining whether the movement's objectives will be achieved or not is the "membership strength" of the movement, and whether or not the membership strength is increasing or decreasing. In these studies, "membership strength" does not refer to the number of people who are mere members of an organization, or who know about it and wish it well. The term refers to the number of people who are rooted in the movement's foundational documents and ideas, whose identity is attached to the movement, who own the movement's driving beliefs and values, and who invest time, energy, and funds for the movement's causes.[10] That understanding of "membership strength" matters, and it matters to churches, and more indicators of that kind of strength are available than we have traditionally used.

The brilliant feature of a more expansive set of

measures is that you can choose the indicators that fit your church's emphasis and philosophy, you can define the terms to fit your philosophy, and you can even weight the indicators to fit your philosophy. One church, for instance, might consider six of the indicators: membership, worship attendance, new Christians, small group attendance, people in lay ministry, and people in cross-cultural mission involvement. To reflect its emphasis, it might weight the worship attendance times two, the small group attendance and the lay ministry involvement times three, and the new Christians received and the lay mission involvement by times ten! It would then add the six numbers (as weighted), and then divide by six, and that dividend would serve as the church's "Approximate Membership Strength Indicator." That dividend is only an approximate indicator of strength to be sure, but a church whose dividend is 20 percent higher than a year ago is experiencing something vastly different than a church whose dividend is 20 percent less than a year ago!

The church with a clear vision, mission, and priorities with objectives that it intends to achieve, and wants to track and plan its progress with rigor worthy of the mission, will find a locally customized set of membership strength indicators to be an invaluable tool for future effectiveness.

E. Find out "WOTS UP." WOTS UP is an acronym for the known Weaknesses, Opportunities, Threats, and Strengths that will Underlie your Planning. Indeed, the main purpose of all of the focused research suggested above, studying the community's demographics and cultures and the church's type and membership strength trends, is not to learn everything possible about the church and the community, but to clearly identify the Threats and (especially) the Opportunities in the community, and the Weaknesses and (especially) the Strengths in the church, that will inform your planning.

When a church discovers a match between a strength in ministry and an opportunity in the community, its leaders are called especially at that point to strategize for outreach. For example, many churches on the west coast of Florida are very experienced and effective in ministries to retired persons; these churches are strategically positioned to reach great numbers of persons now retiring and moving to Florida retirement communities, as well as the "snowbirds" who live in Florida for several months each winter, while retaining their residence "back home." One Florida church discovered that, with its many members from Michigan, it could reach many more retirees and snowbirds from Michigan. Another Florida west coast church is widely regarded as the city's "Buckeye church"! Several Florida churches, with available adult Sunday school classroom space as a strength, have proliferated new adult Sunday school classes—one for Buckeyes, one for Hoosiers, and so forth.

Planning, then, is based on available relevant data; but, important as it is, planning is not an end in itself, but an indispensable means to the meaningful and productive work of the people of the organization, and the achievement of the organization's mission. Appley insisted that every employee know the "big picture" of the company's purpose and goals, and the way in which his or her own tasks contribute to attaining those goals. A classic story in management lore, perhaps apocryphal, involves Michelangelo observing two bricklayers, one doing plodding sluggish work, the other doing inspired enthusiastic work, singing as he worked. Michelangelo asked the plodding worker "What are you doing?" He replied, peevishly, "I am laying one brick on top of another!" To the same question, the enthused worker replied, "We are building a cathedral!"

The effectiveness of any organization depends upon each member knowing the goal toward which the organization is moving, the overall plan for attaining the goal, and how the member's work contributes to the plan. Churches are no exception. In stagnant, conflicted churches one typically observes various groups and factions riding off in various directions and pursuits. In growing effective churches, the various groups spend much of their time and energy pulling together, within a plan, to achieve common objectives.

Chapter Six:
Strategic Planning for Church Growth

Donald McGavran, founder of the Church Growth movement, studied growing and nongrowing churches on every continent for decades. He became a champion of *planning* for the future growth of churches. He observed, across the theological spectrum, that most church leaders assume that church growth will take place without planning, or even without special effort, merely as an indirect outcome of faithful ministry.

Serious readers of this book already know enough to share McGavran's judgment that this assumption is naive. Sooner or later, the sustained growth of any church requires additional seating, ministries, programing, and worship services, which requires additional staffing, facilities, leaders, and lay ministries, all of which emerge through planning and not without it. Furthermore, a church or a denomination serving a ministry area of fifty thousand people with many different people groups will not engage, reach, and serve empty nesters, deaf people, Hispanic immigrants, and gambling addicts without planning. Indeed, McGavran contended, "An adequate plan . . . should make becoming a disciple of Christ a real option to every one of the fifty thousand. No plan is adequate which aims at creating a tiny enclave of two hundred. . . . Church leaders should beware of petty plans."[1] So, McGavran advo-cated "bold plans" for church growth.

In *To Spread the Power: Church Growth in the Wesleyan Spirit,* I ventured the following case for church planning:

> I have observed no church experiencing sustained growth where there was not also an informed strategic plan being implement-ed and with widespread ownership. Although most churches have many plans, those plans are not at the service of a master plan, so the church stagnates and waffles, attempting to ride off in many directions at once. There is a line of questioning that a people must answer together before a stagnant or declining church can experience renaissance: If your church gets where it's going, where will it be? What will this church be like when it grows up? Describe this church as you intend it to be ten years from now. In the words of Galsworthy, "If you do not think about the future, you cannot have one." Robert Schuller states similarly, "If you fail to plan, you plan to fail." Historian Page Smith, a student of movements, tells us that "The leader with a system, however inadequate it may ultimately turn out to be, is at a vast advantage over a systemless rival, however brilliant."[2]

More recently, a stimulating book by Lyle Schaller con-tends your church can, and should, "create your own future!"[3] Schaller observes that churches typically think about their future in one of three ways. (1) Some church leaders, drawing from the obvious life cycle that humans experience, assume a "life cycle" model of their church's history that involves an early growth phase, followed by a maintenance phase, and then by a decline phase. So, once your church is in the decline phase, like fate, there is not much you can do about it. (2) Some church leaders "are convinced that God has prepared a detailed plan for every one of His churches and there is little that mere human beings can do to alter that plan" (p. 12). (3) Some church leaders, however, believe that God has given people, and churches, a range of freedom filled with choices, and Schaller claims that "a worshiping community is not bound by the same constraints of a life cycle that limits the choices available to mere human beings" (p. 12).

Schaller's *Create Your Own Future!* emphasizes the crucial importance of "creating" the "futures committee" that will define the church's future and chart its course.[4] Schaller is adamant about who should not serve on that committee—like people who are in denial about the church's problems, people who oppose the current pastor, people who cannot affirm the church's strengths, people who want to return to the 1950s, and "the individual who insists on recreating 1914 and making this into a geographical parish designed to serve those people who live within walking distance of the church property."[5]

Furthermore, Schaller suggests, the committee should not be essentially a "representative" committee from across the church. Such a committee is, almost invariably, too large, too focused on problems, and too inclined toward "least common denominator compromises." Once formed, the effective futures committee will collaborate with people across the church, and it will keep the church fully informed, but the members should not be selected as a "representative" group.

Who, then, should compose the futures committee? If a viable future for the church will require some discontinuity with its past, the committee should be composed of only seven people who fit the following "Top Ten" traits.[6]

1. Essential agreement on the nature and mission of a Christian church
2. Common perceptions of this congregation's strengths and limitations
3. Agreement on political realities within the church and the need for trade-offs

4. Supportive of the current pastor
5. Looked to by other people as leaders
6. Able and willing to initiate, lead, and even take risks
7. Strong future orientation
8. Convinced that the best days in this church's history are in the future
9. Comfortable in abstract discussions around purpose and mission
10. Active volunteers in the church's life and ministry

George Barna's book *Turning Vision into Action* is one of a flurry of books on the importance of what President Bush once called "the vision thing." Barna does not, however, repeat the mistake of several authors who are so fascinated with the current (re)discovery of "vision" that they assume "vision," by itself, will turn the tide and make the mega-difference. He features the role of "macro-visionaries" (vis-à-vis "micro-visionaries" and "mezzo-visionaries") in creating change. He perceives the futility of discussing "vision" apart from the "values" that shape and drive our lives. The book's driving thesis, that vision needs to be expressed in action, implies the management process for moving from vision to action, and especially the planning process within it.

Much undeserved mystique surrounds "planning." The American Management Association's definition of planning is, essentially, quite simple: Planning is "determining what should be done, how it should be done, where action should be taken, who should be responsible for it, and why."[7] Planning theorists generally divide planning into two types based upon time projection: Planning for the years ahead, for the whole organization, is called strategic planning. Planning for the weeks ahead, for each ministry, activity, and program, is called operational planning.

The strategic planning perspective recognizes that the activity of planning—that is, people deliberating on the future they intend to achieve—is even more important than the written plans that result. The verb counts more than the noun! Process is even more important than product. Likewise, the product—the written plan—is not the goal; the plan is the means to clarifying and (especially) achieving the goals of the church's mission. Too many written plans sit on shelves collecting dust and are never implemented! The process, which I am suggesting is so important, is often broken down into the following seven steps in strategic planning literature. I have seen this process, with slight variations, in more than enough churches to recommend it to every church that wants to be serious about the future.

Step One: Situation Analysis

The strategic planning process, necessarily, begins with an audit, or inventory, or situation analysis—to which the previous chapter was devoted. Future-oriented churches become informed, and frequently updated, on the trends, threats, and opportunities within the wider community, and they become very clear about the church's position within the community and its strengths, weaknesses, and opportunities.

Step Two: Clarifying the Strategic Framework

This step is semi-optional; it may not be logically necessary, but it is usually psychologically necessary. This three part step warms up the committee for the planning process to come, and it helps prepare people in the whole church to contribute to, own, and carry out the plans when developed.

First, often in a meeting or two, the committee clarifies the four to six "Key Result Areas" (KRA) in which the church is not experiencing the outcomes it believes it is called to achieve. So, for example, the committee may want more effectiveness in ministry with young families or deaf people or alcoholics or the church's involvement in world mission.

Second, the committee identifies the church's "stakeholders," defined as all of the people—members, constituents, financial contributors, and so forth—who have a strong "stake" in what the church becomes and achieves. You develop a roster of those people now, because the committee members will be collaborating with those people in the weeks, or months, of the planning process.

Third, the committee may want to clarify afresh the values that they hope will drive the church into the future. For example, Grace United Methodist Church in Minneapolis recently "deemphasized" the denominational label and started presenting the church to the public simply as Grace Church. Using the word GRACE as an acronym, the church's brochure, advertisements, and answering machine explain to the community what the church stands for:

> Grounded in Scripture
> Relevant to the culture
> Authentic in self-presentation
> Compassionate ministries
> Empowered by the Holy Spirit

Step Three: The Mission Statement

The development of a mission statement is the most indispensable step in the strategic planning process. This step, most of all, is fueled by collaboration with the church's stakeholders. Lawrence Appley once suggested that "Planning is a mental clarification process. The best planning takes place when participation by all is secured. The best is that which comes from the bottom up in an organization."[8]

More recent planning literature stresses three reasons for a planning style that collaborates with all the people: (1) You get more and better data, and more and better ideas, when you include all the people. (2) People have greater understanding, and stronger emotional support, of plans that they helped to develop. (3) Collaboratively developed plans, which the people understand and own, are much less likely to be sabotaged and much more likely to be owned and implemented.

The purpose for developing a mission statement is, quite simply, to determine the organization's identity, supreme purpose, major direction, and essential mission for, say, the next five years. A strong mission statement will become the "driving force" of the organization, shaping decisions, impacting budget priorities, and keeping the church on course over time. What kind of mission statement can have that kind of influence? Strategic planning scholars tell us that effective mission statements are:

1. Brief (no more than one hundred words, and preferably much less)
2. Simple
3. General
4. Memorable
5. Energizing

Some scholars add that the mission statement should answer three questions: (1) What? (2) For whom? (3) How? The futures committee and the people may generate dozens of possible mission statements. As the committee gravitates toward one statement, it may write fifty drafts before the statement shines and is ready to fly.

Sometimes, effective mission statements even take the form of mottoes or slogans, which can be used in public relations, as in Dupont's "Better things for better living through chemistry." But the primary audience for a mission statement is internal, not external. Its function is to shape and drive the priorities, decisions, and activities of the organization's people.

The following mission statements from churches serve as examples:

1. To know him and to make him known. (Shepherd of the Valley Lutheran Church, Phoenix, Arizona)

2. That all may know Jesus Christ and become his empowered followers, we share his love with joy, inspired by the Holy Spirit. (Community Church of Joy, Glendale, Arizona)

3. We glorify God in all we do by winning, discipling, and serving. (Frazer Memorial United Methodist Church, Montgomery, Alabama)

4. Loving the people of Cincinnati into relationship with Jesus Christ, serving together, we evangelize to bring God's love in practical ways to all kinds of people; we exalt to celebrate God's presence in fun, culture-current, biblical models; we encourage to develop relationships with God and others; we empower to deepen understanding of Jesus and inspire response to him. (Vineyard Community Church, Cincinnati, Ohio)

5. Our mission is to help irreligious people become fully devoted followers of Jesus Christ. (Willow Creek Community Church, South Barrington, Illinois)

Years ago, when I served on the board of Win Arn's Institute for American Church Growth, I was impressed by the focus and clarity of the Institute's mission statement:

> Believing that the call of God to make disciples is our greatest privilege and responsibility, it shall be the purpose of the Institute to do research and to publicize Church Growth, to discover and disseminate those insights and principles which will enable churches, groups of churches, and denominations in North America to achieve their full potential in making disciples.

Step Four: Determining Missional Objectives

Clear objectives, defined as "the outcomes we want and intend to achieve," are crucial to the effectiveness of any organization, especially a church. (Without driving purposes, the congregation is merely tradition driven—perpetuating a past way of "doing church," often the way they did church in the 1950s.) An effective organization of people is managed through clear, salient objectives. A whole school of thought—Management By Objectives (MBO)—features this idea. A steady fix on objectives helps a church to know whether its mission is being achieved, and a steadfast fix on objectives prevents the church from drifting off course, or slipping into the activity trap. The objectives flow from the mission statement, are consistent with it, and begin to turn strategic planning from a general process into a more specific process.

For example, the mission statement of Shepherd of the Valley Lutheran Church—"To know Him and to make

Him known"—clearly implies two objectives: (1) To know God, and (2) To make God known. For years, the church periodically appraised every ministry, program, activity, and group in the church to see which were serving at least one of those objectives. The leaders eliminated activities that did not, and would not, serve one or both of those objectives!

In time, Shepherd of the Valley's leaders saw the need to develop more, and somewhat more specific, objectives for people. They want the church's ministries, programs, and so forth, to help people to

1. Get Right!
2. Grow Right!
3. Go Right!, and
4. Glow Right!

In the "Get Right" objective, Shepherd of the Valley's leaders want people to get right with God, to understand and realize their justification by grace through faith and be reconciled to God. In the "Grow Right" objective they want people to be informed by scripture and theology. The "Go Right" objective focuses on involving people in lay ministries and in local evangelistic outreach and cross-cultural mission. The "Glow Right" objective centers on developing Christians of depth and contagion through spiritual formation.

Step Five: Setting Goals for Each Objective

The strategic planning process moves from general (the mission statement) to somewhat more specific (the objectives within the mission) to still more specific— the goals for each objective. Each objective should be matched with one or more goals—yes, numerical goals.

Admittedly, the achievement of an organization's numerical goals may not be supremely important. The achievement of the organization's objectives is very important, however; and the goals that are related to each objective provide the indicators that enable us to know whether or not we are achieving our mission objectives. Setting goals, for which the leaders hold themselves accountable, is therefore a crucial variable in strategic planning for church growth.

A quarter century ago, Peter Wagner and Virgil Gerber led week-long church growth seminars in Latin America. In the last session of each seminar, the instructors gave participants the opportunity to set growth goals for the next year and to agree to report to the follow-up seminar scheduled for the next year. Some participants set goals and some did not, but all participants had the same training. One year later, participants who had not set goals were only slightly more likely to have experienced church growth than churches whose leaders had not even attended the first church growth seminar; the churches whose leaders did set growth goals, however, were much more likely to have experienced significant church growth.

How do you engage in effective goal setting? How does a group of leaders go about setting goals? Through extensive experience in many organizations, a proven set of principles, or criteria, can guide us in catalytic goal setting. Lyle Schaller suggests that the acronym SAM can help us recall that effective goals are (at least) (1) Specific, (2) Attainable, and (3) Measurable. Two other criteria are often employed. (4) Ownership: An effective goal has the ownership of the people who will be needed to implement it. (5) Scheduled: If a goal does not have a target date for its completion, with scheduled milestones toward its completion, it may not be a goal that the leaders intend to achieve!

The first and third criteria, specific and measurable, carry rather obvious meaning and usefulness. For example, if I told a friend that I am going to "Lose some weight," the friend might say "Hunter, that is only a wish; it is not a goal that you intend to achieve in measurable time." However, if I stated the goal of losing ten pounds in the next two months--that is sufficiently specific and measurable to suggest that I might be serious!

Current discussion around the "attainable" criterion for good goals, however, involves three different perspectives. One perspective projects what we are achieving now into the future. So, if our worship attendance this year averaged 150 and we reached 10 new people, we feel that averaging 155 and reaching 11 new people would be attainable next year. Many churches set growth goals that are so modest that they can probably achieve their goals without depending upon the third person of the Trinity! The subtle spiritual effect on such church leaders, over time, is quietly devastating.

So, a contrasting perspective suggests a second guideline: "Attainable with Stretch." Healthy organizations want their people's efforts to be appreciably more productive next year than this year. Churches, especially, should set goals that are plausible, but which probably would not be achieved unless the living God attended and empowered their efforts. Leaders in this perspective want to exceed the goals they set, because they value the "momentum" that comes from exceeding its goals, and they fear the withdrawal from future goal setting that sets in when the church achieves short of its goals.

A third perspective is reflected in the splendid book by Jim Collins and Jerry Porras, *Built to Last*.[9] That landmark study is probably the most important study of effective organizations since Thomas J. Peters and Robert H. Waterman's *In Search of Excellence* published in the early 1980s. Collins and Porras studied perennially great organizations vis-à-vis comparable organizations (contributing similar products or services) that were merely good organizations. They identified several principles that separated the great organizations from the merely good ones. For one thing, the great "visionary" organizations are often driven by "BHAG"—an acronym for **Big Hairy Audacious Goals**! Since *Built to Last* was published, some churches have adopted "BHAG," projecting significantly more growth than they'd been experiencing before.

For example, the largest church in Lexington, Kentucky, where I live, is Southland Christian Church. Several years ago, Wayne Smith, the founding pastor and a popular engaging folk preacher, announced his retirement. Many people assumed that Smith would be impossible to follow. The search committee imported Mike Breaux from a church in Las Vegas. Breaux, with some resistance, repositioned Southland from a traditional seeker sensitive church to a contemporary seeker driven church. The leaders developed a mission statement:

> "To connect unconnected people to Jesus Christ,
> and together grow in full devotion to Him."

In less than a year, the two morning services were full. Southland was receiving more than three hundred new Christians per year. The leaders added a Saturday evening service, and they plan a second. They moved the sleepy Sunday evening service, which averaged 50 to 100, to a Wednesday night Encounter service for believers that now averages 1,000. In the three years of Mike Breaux's tenure, Southland's weekend attendance has grown from 3,400 to over 6,000.

As Southland's leaders noticed some people leaving by the backdoor, however, they developed clearer objectives around outreach, discipleship, and community.

Believing that expanding the small group life is the best way to close the backdoor, the church now projects two "BHAG"—300 groups meeting weekly and 10,000 people in weekend attendance, within five years.

Willow Creek Community Church is projecting the biggest, hariest, most audacious goals of any church I know. In 1996, building upon their first 20 years, Willow Creek's people set the following BHAG to achieve by the end of A.D. 2000:

	1996	Goal for 2001
Weekend Attendance	14,326	20,000
Midweek New Community Attendance	4,661	8,000
People Involved in Small Groups	8,000	20,000
Participating Membership	1,465	8,000
Laity in Ministries Beyond the Church	771	4,000
Member Churches in the Willow Creek Association	1,400	6,000

As you compare the six goals with each other in terms of the percentage growth they project, they are all ambitious, but some are less "hairy" and "audacious" than the others, and several are more than audacious! This illustrates that goals are affected by variables like changes in philosophy, the history of the emphasis, and available facilities. For example, the weekend attendance goal approaches the maximum that Willow Creek's seating capacity could accommodate in five weekend services; the midweek New Community attendance goal approaches the maximum capacity in two weeknight services. The projected 150 percent growth in small group involvement reflects Willow Creek's shift in the early 1990s from being a church with small groups to a church of small groups, and their extravagant projection in lay ministry involvement beyond the church reflects an amplified emphasis in the church's philosophy of ministry. The increase in membership reflects Willow Creek's clarification of what they mean by "church membership" and their increased capacity to assimilate new people in a group and deploy them in a ministry. The projected increase in the Willow Creek Association was made in an early period of the Association's history, but with enough history to know the growing interest in the Association.

How is Willow Creek doing in fulfilling their "BHAG"? As this is written, the church is halfway into the five-year plan. The average weekend attendance is now 16,505, and the New Community is averaging almost 6,000. The membership stands at 4,700, and 13,850 people are involved in small groups. Member churches (and other organizations) in the Willow Creek Association now number 3,674.

Step Six: Strategies

A strategy is the broad action that an organization will take to move toward achieving an objective. Typically, an informed planning group will identify a range of possible strategies, from which they will run with the most promising several strategies, which they will execute in tandem.

The chief contribution of the Church Growth movement's field research has been to identify the strategic directions that churches typically follow that lead to significant growth. A half century of research has produced more strategic conclusions than any one writer has adequately summarized. For our purposes in this book, I can summarize, at the generic level, three strategies from Church Growth strategic lore that contribute to growth wherever we find it.[10]

I. Identifying and Reaching Receptive People

This principle partly rests on the commonplace observation that, at any given time, some people are more receptive to a proposal that they buy a car or enter a degree program or get married or adopt a faith than other people, *and* that the same person may be more (or less) receptive this year than last year. Donald McGavran emphasized that receptivity to the Christian faith "ebbs and flows" in persons, and among peoples. Therefore, he counseled, when we observe that many people in a given society are receptive, we must be aware that the conditions through which God's prevenient grace is working to awaken their responsiveness will not last forever, so the mission must gather this harvest while it is harvesttime. Church Growth strategy calls for deploying disproportionate numbers of missionaries in fields that are "ripe for the harvest," and for identifying and reaching the most receptive people within each field. Indeed, Church Growth research has gradually developed a set of "indicators" for finding responsive people:[11]

1. Pre-Christian people who are linked, by kinship or friendship, to credible Christians (especially new Christians) are more receptive than other people.

2. People are more receptive to outreach from new groups, classes, worship services, and churches than from long established ones.

3. People are more responsive to churches with ministries that engage their felt needs.

4. People are more receptive to a church whose style, language, and music is indigenous to their culture than to a church employing forms alien to their culture.

5. Many people in a population in which any religion is growing are open and searching for something.

6. People among whom any religion has experienced decline tend to be receptive.

7. A people experiencing major culture change tend to be receptive.

8. People experiencing population mobility, like the people in a new settlement, are often receptive.

9. In most seasons, in most nations, the "masses" are more receptive than the "classes."

10. People who are "like" the active members of a church, especially its new members, tend to be

more receptive than the surrounding population as a whole.

11. People who are dissatisfied with themselves, or with their life, are often open to something else.

12. People experiencing important life transitions are more receptive than people in stability.

13. Visitors to a church's worship service are frequently receptive to that church—for a short period of time.

Any church's planning group will find at least several of those indicators relevant to their ministry area. Indeed, an informed use of the indicators will usually help them find more receptive people than they ever dreamed were out there! Nevertheless, this approach should not be interpreted as a secular "map" for finding receptive people; it is more of a guide for prayer. Ultimately, the churches that pray to be led to receptive people keep discovering such people by "coincidence"!

II. Outreach Across Social Networks

This principle, reflected in Donald McGavran's earliest book, *The Bridges of God*,[12] suggests that (contrary to widespread evangelical myth) the faith does not spread between strangers, or from mass evangelism or media evangelism, but rather between relatives, friends, and neighbors. Kinship and friendship networks provide "the Bridges of God." Win and Charles Arn have observed that the faith spread this way in New Testament times, and they call it the *oikos* principle. Translators usually translate *oikos* with the English term "household," but the Arns show that, in addition to one's family, the term (and the social experience behind it) could include a range of intimates like close friends, slaves, frequent trading partners, and so forth. In their studies of contemporary church growth in America, the Arns declare that "webs of common kinship (the larger family), common friendship (friends and neighbors), and common associates (special interests, work relationships, and recreation) are still the paths most people follow in becoming Christians today." With some variation by region, culture, and class, 75 percent to 90 percent of all converts report a friend or relative as the one factor most responsible for their joining.[13]

Many strategic churches experience sustained growth by implementing this principle. Each season, they first collect the names of the unchurched people in the social networks of their active members and especially those of their new members. Then they invite these people to small group meetings, pastor's classes, special worship services, and so forth, and they get in conversation with those who are responsive. As some of them profess faith and join, the church reaches out to their unchurched friends and relatives.

III. The Multiplication of Recruiting Units

This generic principle of church growth applies to every area and level of the church's life. Churches starting new Sunday school classes tend to have a growing Sunday school. Churches starting new men's groups tend to have a growing men's ministry. Churches starting new youth groups tend to have a growing youth ministry. Churches that start new worship services tend to have a growing worship attendance. Judicatories and denominations that are starting new churches tend to grow.

There appear to be at least two principles involved in these correlations between new units and growth. First, the more units you have recruiting and welcoming people, the greater membership strength you experience. So, for example, you would reasonably expect a church with five choirs (or singing ensembles) to involve more people in the choral music ministry than a church with one choir, you would expect a church with five services to involve more people per weekend than an otherwise comparable church with a single service, and you would expect a denomination with 5,000 churches to report more members than a denomination with 1,000 churches.

Second, new groups are more reproductive than old units, so it matters how many (and what percentage) of your units are new. For example, in the local church examples cited above, not every unit will thrive. Two out of every ten new choirs or singing ensembles may not endure; three out of ten new services may not find a lasting constituency; and four out of ten new Sunday school classes, youth groups, and men's groups may not make it for a year. But the groups, services, ensembles, and choirs that do make it will bring in a very large percentage of the new people.

In regard to whole churches, we consider a church to be "new" for about the first fifteen years of its life. With many exceptions and irregularities to be sure, many "well-planted" churches average growing about 10 percent per year for the first 15 years before they kind of "naturally plateau." Now, The United Methodist Church (with about 35,000 churches), and the Southern Baptist Convention (with about 41,000 churches), are apparently in the same "league" in overall denominational strength. However, if I told you that only about 1,000 United Methodist churches are in that first-generation growth track, and about 9,000 Southern Baptist churches, you would not be astonished to learn that The United Methodist Church is experiencing net decline and the Southern Baptist Convention is experiencing net growth!

Step Seven: Ministries, Activities, and Programs

From strategic planning's historic roots in the strategic thinking of military leaders, writers often refer to this step as "tactics," which is defined as the specific programs and activities (and, for churches, ministries) for implementing the strategy. Unfortunately, many churches begin at the level of tactics, skipping the first six steps in the process.

For example, one church built a Family Life Center, not because they decided that their mission was to nuclear families with children and youth, but because a staff person decided she would enjoy running one. Another church built a Family Life Center because the "most avant garde churches are now building family life centers." Another church recruited and equipped a "handbell choir," not because handbell music is an indigenous music genre to an unreached population, but because "First Church" has a handbell choir, and a church matriarch provided for one in her will. The examples could proliferate.

The point is that most churches develop a patchwork of random programs and activities, and then resource and staff them, out of many interests and agendas—to the exclusion of a conscious mission strategy. More than eight of every ten churches in North America have no informed plan for their future that involves reaching pre-Christian people, that is being implemented in decisions about ministries and programming.

Indeed, the history of many churches is essentially the story of an extensive patchwork of "mere programs"—each program once championed by a special interest faction or funded in a will or modeled by a megachurch or imported from denominational headquarters or imposed by the judicatory or denominational hierarchy. Many of these programs achieved something for a season and then declined. The church has subsidized and perpetuated the programs ever since, even though they no longer achieve their original purpose, even though their leaders no longer recall the original purpose, even though we would never choose to start them today if they were not already in place. The programs bloomed only briefly, and then drifted, because they were not expressing a strategy in the service of a clear objective within a mission.

Operational Planning

The planning done for ministries, activities, and programs is called operational planning. Operational planning basically answers the questions of (1) Who will (2) do what (3) by when? Most churches are competent at operational planning for a church program or activity, and at recording the agreements to the three questions in minutes, so there is no need in this book to elaborate on operational planning. Most churches need to add competence in strategic planning to their competence in operational planning.

As we conclude this consideration of strategic planning, I am more aware than ever that a crucial question faces most church leaders: "Am I willing to become a strategic leader?" Likewise, a crucial question faces most churches: "Are we willing to become a strategic church?"

Most church people assume that "strategy" belongs exclusively in the thinking of military, political, and business leaders. Indeed, the root meaning of "strategy" is "the art of generalship," or, expanded, "the science and art of employing all means available in the planning and direction of large scale operations."[14] Clearly, a government's response to terrorism or an industry's challenge of marketing Chevrolets in China or a campaign committee's challenge of electing an unknown candidate to the Senate would, necessarily, involve strategic thinking. But the church's leaders, generally, do not think of achieving the objectives of the church's mission in strategic terms.

However, the historic Christian movement has had its fair share of strategic thinkers—such as Paul, Saint Patrick, Pope Gregory, John Wesley, Charles Grandison Finney, William and Catherine Booth, and, in our own time, Donald McGavran and Ralph Winter. When we face the complexity of the unfinished missionary task—reaching three billion unreached people, in some twelve thousand different people groups, speaking over four thousand different languages and dialects, we see that strategic thinking is needed for Christianity's world mission. Indeed, virtually every community today is a complex local mission field, characterized by such secularization, population diversity, accelerating change, and human needs as to require more strategic thinking than most church leaders have yet imagined, much less practiced.

The basic issue facing church leaders in every community is whether they can be content with merely providing chaplain services for the people who are already Christians, or whether they are called by the Holy Spirit to become an apostolic movement among nonbelievers. Leaders who feel drawn to the latter option will find themselves dreaming some radical dreams, and called to a level of analysis, planning, and strategic thinking that is not (yet) characteristic of many churches.

Chapter Seven:
Organizing People and Resources to Achieve the Church's Apostolic Purpose

The United Methodist Church's membership strength in the U.S., and that of most other mainline ("old line" or "sideline") denominations, has declined for the last three decades. In the late 1970s, the annual rate of decline was decreasing, and the extended graph showed the denomination "bottoming out" by the early to mid 1930s. But the annual decline rate increased again, and now the end of decline is not in sight. So, in recent years, United Methodism's decline has become the object of much hand-wringing and the subject of analysis, episcopal attention, and prophetic books.[1]

One important conclusion is now widely acknowledged—multiple causes lie behind the membership decline of any local church or any denomination. It follows, therefore, that no one intervention is going to turn things around, and every grab for a "quick fix" is futile. But such realism has produced, in some folks, despair—the feeling that the decline's causes are so mysterious and complex we can never fathom it, much less fix it. Some "leaders" are even resigned to Methodism's perpetual decline and advise us to "make the best of it." But, the causes of United Methodism's decline are not as mysterious as we think, and serious strategic interventions at two levels, informed by two simple questions, would advance the possibility of United Methodism, and other mainline denominations, regaining momentum in the U.S. once again. The two questions are raised in the following story.

> People were gathering in a mortuary chapel for the funeral of a beloved Methodist grandmother. The undertaker opened the casket; to his astonishment, the grandmother's body was not there. The casket contained the body of a three-star general in full uniform. The undertaker panicked and telephoned the morgue, explaining "We must have the right body here in fifteen minutes." The morgue director consulted their computer and replied, "Go ahead and bury the body you have now. The grandmother was buried yesterday—with full military honors!" The chuckle in this case hinges on two questions: *Where in the world was that Methodist grandmother?* and *What was she doing there?*

Much of the United Methodist Church's track record, and that of many other old-line denominations, hinges on two similar questions: Where are our people? and What are they doing there? Management gurus tell us that the performance and destiny of any organization hangs largely on how the leaders answer those questions. Effective organizations have leaders who know where to deploy their people, who are clear on what they want their people to be doing and achieving. Ineffective organizations have leaders who do not strategically deploy their people to achieve the organization's main business.

For churches too, where and how we deploy our people influences the effectiveness of our whole mission, including our rate of membership growth or decline. This principle can be demonstrated at every level of The United Methodist Church's life. For instance, at the world level, the UMC now places only one missionary for every 23,000 members; by comparison, a dozen North American denominations place more than one missionary for every 1,000 members! Furthermore, most of the UMC's missionaries are not employed primarily for apostolic work; most of them serve the institutions of the existing Church in various lands. (They teach in a college, manage a clinic, teach English as a second language, or work in community development, and so forth.) These facts help explain why the UMC's mission agency has not within memory launched many new growing movements among unreached peoples of the earth.

At the national level, one supreme (but widely ignored) reason for the denomination's net membership decline is that, in a century of great urbanization, the UMC is not structured to be an urban movement; it still distributes its churches and deploys its ministers to reach the population as it used to be scattered across the hinterland, rather than how the people are increasingly "stacked" in our cities. So, the UMC now rather typically places a church and a minister for every 3,000 to 4,000 people in rural counties and a church and minister for every 30,000 to 40,000 in urban counties. In considering church growth at every level, it matters where you deploy your people and what you ask them to do.

At the level of local churches and communities, the deployment principle reveals a very major cause of the net membership decline of thousands of United Methodism's local churches. How a congregation deploys its staff and (especially) its volunteers strongly influences its growth rate. For instance, a pastor visiting unchurched people in the community will attract more people into the faith than will a pastor spending priority time and energy on meetings, judicatory matters, office work, and ecclesiastical chores. Hire a new staff person for an outreach ministry, and the church will grow more than if you hire a professional to counsel the members. Deploy volunteers in outreach and ministry to people, and you will grow; deploy them in governance, committee work, maintenance, and "good church work," and your church will decline.

This is why Donald McGavran, father of the Church Growth movement, counseled churches to measure the amount of time they spend on themselves and the amount of time they spend in outreach, and to be "rather ruthless" in that measurement. I have found it equally helpful to use the same analytic exercise in church groups—men's fellowships, women's societies, youth fellowships, Sunday school classes. So, in a local church's mission, it really matters where we deploy people and what we ask them to do. Most churches will grow if they spend as much time and energy on outreach as they spend on maintenance.

The question of staffing for growth becomes especially crucial for breaking "the 200 barrier." One pastor and a part-time secretary can manage a church of 150 to 200 in average worship attendance, though the church at that strength is staffed for maintenance, not for growth. Though much research needs to be done on the staffing practices of growing churches, the following generalizations are defensible:

First, growing churches hire more laypeople and more part-time people than stagnant and declining churches do. These churches perceive, in their churches and communities, a growing number of educated, capable, devoted laypeople—such as mothers with children at home, retired military officers, and other capable people who took early retirement from their first vocation, who are very available for meaningful part-time employment in the cause of Christ. Indeed, growing churches are way ahead of secular organizations in shaping meaningful roles that competent part-time people can fill.

Second, the earlier practice of expanding staff largely by hiring more and more ordained associate pastors appears to be dying out; growing churches now seem to employ pastors only for those roles in which ordination and/or advanced theological education is indispensable. At the same time, growing churches rely so heavily on the associate ministers they do employ that they employ proven associates with experience rather than recent seminary graduates who will be leaving for their own church in three years. Furthermore, growing churches regard their career associate pastors with much higher status than do traditional maintenance churches.

Third, growing churches tend to pay their people well—consistent with, and sometimes exceeding, what their competency could earn in a secular job.

Fourth, the effective senior minister, in his or her "rancher" role, assigns a (once unimaginable) level of freedom and responsibility to staff persons, with the authority to match the responsibility. Staff people have clear outcomes to work for in their area of responsibility, and their achievements are rewarded and given public recognition. For example, the senior minister does not take credit for all the good things that happen!

Fifth, growing churches are not immobilized by the myth that it is hard to recruit good staff because they have found it comparatively easy to recruit experienced competent staff. They often find and recruit competent people from staffs of churches where staff are not trusted or given freedom, recognition, and sufficient authority!

Sixth, growing churches do not rely inordinately upon raiding other staffs. They more often develop their own laypeople into staff roles, and they provide for the continued development of staff people. They even budget for books, training, and continuing education.

Seventh, the staff functions as a team, in which policies and decisions are developed collaboratively, which models the collaborative style in which each staff person works with the lay officers and volunteers in his/her sphere of responsibility.

Eighth, growing churches staff for growth, not maintenance. For example, they do not first announce a new singles ministry, get a hundred singles involved, and then hire a director of singles ministries. They know, in the age-old controversy of "which comes first," that the chicken comes before the eggs.

While effective staffing is crucial for the continued growth of a church, the recruitment and deployment of lay volunteers in various ministries is even more crucial. A local church is, in organization theory terms, a voluntary organization; the most effective churches, therefore, are the most effective in identifying, recruiting, coaching, developing, deploying, and affirming great and growing numbers of lay volunteers. Indeed, the staff persons are "ranchers" (or at least "foremen")—who do ministry, but even more are responsible for recruiting, developing, and involving laypeople in ministry. In such churches, for example, laypeople do most of the (very) regular hospital visitation, much of the counseling, most of the pastoral care, most of the visitation of unchurched people, and most of the visible community involvement. So, every staff person is a "manager" who is employed to get things done through other people.

Growing churches are very unlike traditional maintenance churches in the way they recruit and deploy volunteers. They are opposed to "filling slots" or forcing square pegs into round holes. Indeed, they refuse to put lay volunteers into roles for which they are not gifted. Rather, they (1) first work to identify a person's aptitudes or spiritual gifts for ministry and then place the person in a task or role suited to the perceived gifts; sometimes, they even build a job around someone's spiritual gifts for ministry.[2] (2) Effective growing churches intentionally provide training, feedback, and coaching when someone takes on a new job. (3) They ensure that each person in a job knows what kinds of outcomes to work for and how their job fits into the overall plan and mission of the congregation. (4) They say "thank you" and give public recognition to people doing a faithful effective job, and they engage in other expressions of positive reinforcement and public modeling of the mission of the laity. (5) Such churches, like other effective organizations, work for what Appley calls "organization clarification"—which means "that anyone who has supervision over others should make sure those people understand: 1. What their *functions* are. 2. What *authority* goes with those functions. 3. What *relationships* they have with others."[3]

While the church has its own distinctive identity and mission, and it would therefore be inappropriate to simply copy a corporation or business, nevertheless churches have much to learn from businesses in the management of physical resources, such as buildings, equipment, technology, money, and so forth. In this area, many churches do not think very strategically. For instance, many churches build their buildings first and then decide what they hope to achieve, what staff they need, and so forth! Any effective business executive could have told them that form should follow function.

Even more seriously, many church organizations acquire as much property as possible, build as large a building as possible, and/or assemble as much staff as possible—and then try to achieve their mission. Such church organizations do not realize (early enough) that any property, facility, or staff they do not need to achieve their mission is not an asset, but a liability—something they have to drag along behind them to achieve their mission. The experience of Oral Roberts University (ORU) in the 1980s served as a visible case in point. Oral Roberts aspired to build a great hospital. He believed that "If you build it, they will come—from across the earth!" All of the solicited (and unsolicited) advice that Roberts received counseled him, strongly, against the hospital; there were already too many hospital beds in Tulsa, and people in San Diego or Sao Paulo would not leave their families and local support systems to go to ORU for surgery. Roberts built the hospital anyway, and the ensuing years witnessed one frantic television financial appeal after another to keep the largely empty hospital from sinking the whole university. If you build a facility you do not need to achieve your mission, the facility is not an asset, but a liability.

Also in the 1980s, mission supporters followed the saga of the U.S. Center for World Mission, in Pasadena, California. In 1977, Dr. Ralph Winter, whose dreams for world evangelization founded the center, acquired first buying rights to a campus that the Nazarenes were selling. Winter raised the money for a down payment, moved in, and invited various mission organizations to move in too. Some of the early dreams were realized, but Winter and his staff gave priority energy to raising money for over a decade in order to meet the scheduled payments. Winter's evangelical constituency witnessed years of frantic eleventh-hour financial appeals, and extreme creativity, in dramatizing the center's dream and need for potential donors. It was, and is, more campus than the center's mission needed; the excess has not been experienced as an asset, but as a liability. But many church leaders are unaware of their myopia regarding property and buildings. When I once asked Ralph Winter if the U.S. Center had bit off more property than they could chew, he replied that it was "Not too much, when you consider a whole world in need of Christ!"

Compared to many church organizations, effective businesses and corporations do *not* amass as much property as possible. Their strategy is to achieve as much as possible with as little as possible. The principle is called Return on Investment (ROI) or Return on Invested Capital (ROIC). By this principle, a company with $5,000,000 invested in its capital facilities, which made $1,000,000 last year, and therefore earned an annual return of 20 percent on its invested capital, is a more effective company than another that made $2,000,000 while working from capital assets worth $20,000,000— representing only a 10 percent return on their investment. Lee Iacocca's rightly celebrated turnaround of Chrysler was due, initially, to his rigorous application of the ROIC principle. Chrysler was not selling many more cars after their turnaround than in their earlier decline, but Iacocca had closed or sold some of Chrysler's least productive plants; they were now making and selling more cars from fewer plants (and workers) and were now wildly successful.

What does the ROI principle look like in church organizations? Two cases should clarify the point. If you visited Fuller Theological Seminary's campus, in Pasadena, California, you would never guess that Fuller is one of the five largest theological seminaries in North America. Until it built a handsome facility for its School of Psychology, Fuller featured only several modest buildings, and several renovated houses. What they have— offices, library, post office, bookstore, cafeteria—is adequate and useful, but so much is missing in the usual "campus" paradigm. You look almost in vain to find classrooms, auditoriums, and so forth. The reason?

Fuller rents classroom space in Pasadena churches; the seminary's regular chapel services are at First Presbyterian Church; they hold graduation in First United Methodist Church. Fuller's distinguished long-term president, David Hubbard, practiced the ROIC principle; whenever possible, Fuller would rather pour its endowment income and tuition income into programs and people than into buildings!

Frazer Memorial United Methodist Church in Montgomery, Alabama, has grown in 25 years from fewer than 400 members to more than 7,500 members, from 150 average worship attendance to over 4,500. Throughout its growth history, Frazer has never been obsessed with impressive buildings. They have built facilities, and they have expanded facilities, as needed; but throughout this growth history Frazer has maintained three Sunday morning worship services and three sessions of the Sunday school. Frazer believes in scheduling to achieve more through lesser facilities, rather then building one gigantic facility. Increasingly, the Frazer model appears to be the wave of the future. More and more growing churches cannot afford to continue, or cannot justify continuing, the luxury of building a large enough facility to house everyone in just one worship service and one session of the Sunday school. The greatly growing churches of the Third World herald the same lesson. The Kwang Lim Methodist Church in Seoul, Korea—now world Methodism's largest church with over 60,000 members—serves over 20,000 worshipers a Sunday, distributed among five major worship services. The Yoido Central Full Gospel Church plays to a capacity worship attendance exceeding 20,000—seven times per Sunday!

How a church deploys its human resources and how it plans and uses its physical resources are often decisive factors (in human terms) for whether the church is declining or growing.

Chapter Eight: Delegating Kingdom Work to the People of God—with Performance Standards and Appraisal

I will never forget the first meeting in which my job performance was appraised. I had finished my first year as assistant professor of evangelism, in May of 1973, at Southern Methodist University's Perkins School of Theology. The dean was Joseph D. Quillian, Jr., an aristocratic educator in the old Southern tradition—a Yale Ph.D., an imposing presence, an encyclopedic vocabulary, and a perceptive listener with the memory of an elephant. As I walked toward his office in the administration building, I recalled my first command performance in a dean's office. I was fourteen and had been sent to the dean's office in our high school for gambling during recess. Now, at thirty-five, the same feelings of dread resurfaced.

Joe greeted me warmly, poured two cups of tea, and pulled from a file two copies of the goals for the year I had written the previous September. We read the first goal, and he asked what progress or achievement I could report. We discussed the other several goals in similar specifics. As I recall, Joe affirmed my teaching, my rapport with the students, my involvement in my division and two committees, and my emerging leadership in the church of the region. "However," he said, "I note that you haven't written anything for publication." I suddenly felt defensive, and I asked, "Is the 'publish or perish' doctrine really all it's cracked up to be?" Joe paused; I could tell he saw right through my ploy. He replied, "Chuck, if you are not writing, there is no empirical evidence that you are thinking. Besides, you have so much to offer to the wider church, I will be insisting that you write."

As we finished our meeting, Joe said he needed my written goals for the next year within two weeks. "Those goals," he said, "will serve as the agenda for our meeting next May." He added, "You have had a very good first year. We are glad you came to Perkins. Let us know how we can help you excel." I walked out of my first performance evaluation feeling affirmed and talking to myself: "Joe really does want me to educate apostles, missionaries, evangelists, and witnesses in this student body and beyond. His role is to keep me focused and accountable, and to help me from time to time."

The experience I had feared became an experience I have cherished. Since then, I have led a staff at denominational headquarters for six years and at Asbury Theological Seminary for seventeen. That experience has consistently confirmed what I first saw modeled in Joe Quillian. The effective management of people necessarily involves effective delegation, performance goals, and performance appraisal.

The critical act in achieving the organization's objectives through other people is delegation. Effective leaders typically delegate most of the organization's work to other people; many leaders delegate from ten to fifty specific tasks per day. If the pastor, and other church leaders, do not delegate the preparation of the bulletin, the teaching of Sunday school classes, the visitation of new families in town, the delivery of meals-on-wheels, or a hundred other tasks in the total ministry and mission of a congregation—then the leaders do those tasks themselves (and, therefore, are not really leaders). More likely, most of those important tasks do not get done and the mission is not achieved.

Leaders who do not delegate effectively undermine their own best aspirations, and they unwittingly participate in one or more pathologies. Many church leaders report their reluctance to delegate important assignments and tasks. They "tried it once," the job wasn't done "right," and they say, "It's just easier to do it yourself." But, if we are educable, experience teaches that it is not easier to do everything oneself, and we discover ourselves locked into a script whose last scene ends in burnout. Some leaders harbor exaggerated ideas about their own omnicompetence, or their own indispensability, or they have trouble trusting other people, or they are reluctant to let go of control and give someone the authority that fits the responsibility. Others ("abdicrats") engage in glib or superficial delegating behaviors; they dump it from their desk onto someone else's, and in time are astonished by the anarchy in their organization. Still others appear to delegate a task, but then hover over the shoulder of the other person and immobilize them. The delegation of even a simple task, like "Son, please take out the garbage," can be a complex emotion-charged transaction between two persons.

Clearly, delegation is crucial to the life and achievement of any organization and is important enough to learn to do it effectively. The consensus in management literature focuses on four basic steps in effective delegation: (1) Choosing a capable person, that is, someone with the gifts, competence, and interest. (2) Explaining the desired objectives, results, or outcomes. (3) Giving the person the authority and the resources to do the job;

many church leaders, like Pharaoh of old, expect bricks to be made without straw. (4) Keeping in contact—enough to monitor progress, to be helpful, and to positively reinforce good work, but not such close supervision as to smother the other person.

Obviously, the verbal contract needs to clarify the working relationship between the person delegating and the person who will do the task. Lawrence Appley shares a simple set of options for clarifying the extent of authority being delegated:

1. Act
2. Act and tell
3. Act after consultation
4. Act upon instruction from another[1]

Thousands of tasks, of course, are not explicitly delegated; these tasks go with the job of secretary, Sunday school teacher, worship leader, evangelism committee chair, or hospital visitor. This fact uncovers the greatest human rights violation found in churches and church organizations—the inalienable right of every person who takes a job to have a job description that clarifies the work to be done and the standards that will indicate the work's satisfactory performance.

The collected wisdom regarding job descriptions for people taking jobs in churches and other voluntary organizations includes the following guidelines: (1) Job descriptions should be written. (2) Job descriptions should be brief—one page. (3) The person taking the job should participate substantially in the writing (or rewriting) of the job description; they will then more likely "own," recall, and implement what the job description calls for. (4) The job should, as much as possible, be built upon the person's interests, abilities, experience, likely contribution, and potential for personal development.

(5) Each task in the job description should specify its objectives, that is, the desired outcomes—with measurable standards or indicators of when the job is being done well. (6) The person in a job should refer often to the job description and standards of performance—to stay on course and to avoid indulgences or mere random activity; there should be frequent conversations, based upon the job description and standards, between the person and the manager. Appley remarks that "experience shows that standards of performance may be written for any job. The more definite the job, the more definite and measurable the standards. The more general the job, the greater the results from the development of standards."[2] The plea here is that regardless of the job, an attempt should be made to write standards of performance for it. Each attempt will produce better standards; all attempts will produce better attitudes and better results. Imperfect and immeasurable as they may be, they are still better than none.

As suggested above, a performance oriented job description is a human right, that is, something we owe to every person who works in our church, organization, or cause. Actually, according to the American Management Association, organization leaders owe their people five things: (1) Leaders owe people clear, specific *performance expectations*; otherwise the person has one set of expectations in mind, and the manager another. (2) Leaders owe people realistic *priorities* within the performance expectations. (3) Leaders owe people the necessary *resources* needed to perform, that is, the money, time, tools, information, training, and so forth that are needed to do the job to standard. (4) The leader owes his/her people a focus upon the *results* wanted, not upon methods; good managers let people, particularly people with relevant experience, do it their way. (5) Leaders owe their people *feedback* on their performance.

Feedback, not Wheaties, is "the breakfast of champions." People need to know how they are doing; clear performance standards enable people to know how they are doing without being told.

Larry Knauff, a teacher for the American Management Association, recommends developing performance standards that answer four questions that are especially relevant to churches:

1. What are the key result areas, or the major job responsibilities, of the job? Many times, a church position description lacks this essential clarity. I consulted in a church where there was conflict around the choir leader's job performance. I asked the choir leader, the pastor, and the chairperson of the staff-parish relations committee to each write out their perception of the choir leader's major job responsibilities; I would have never guessed they were describing the same job! When descriptions of church positions like choir director are effective, they generally involve the person in the writing, and they delineate six to ten major job responsibilities, stated in one to four words each; voluntary positions, like Sunday school teacher, have four to six or seven major job responsibilities.

I once challenged the pastors in a Doctor of Ministry class to generate, in five minutes, the likely key result areas in the job description of a Sunday school teacher for elementary-age children. They quickly generated the following: Such a Sunday school teacher would be expected to (a) provide a loving environment in the class; (b) model Christian life, character, and relationships for the children; (c) have the children work with the Scriptures and learn appropriate biblical content and meanings; (d) know the children and their families; (e) increase class size—especially adding children from pre-Christian families; and (f) mold the class into a group, encouraging meaningful membership and relationships. That is not a bad job description for five minutes of group brainstorming, and, while it could stand refining, it is a better map of this important volunteer ministry than 99 percent of all children's Sunday school teachers now have to guide them.

2. How do we measure performance in the job? A job description needs at least one attainable performance indicator that is relevant to what you want achieved, for each key result area. Such indicators function something like batting averages in appraising the performance of a baseball player. A helpful question for developing performance indicators is "What tells me, right now, if I am doing a good job?" My Doctor of Ministry class, in this way, added indicators to the job description of the hypothetical children's Sunday school class teacher: (A) Weekly behavior such as greeting children by name, appropriate touching and hugging, and celebrating birthdays would indicate serious attention to providing a loving environment. (B) Regular worship attendance and graciousness in handling class disruptions would indicate appropriate modeling of Christian lifestyle. (C) The children's own clear and imaginative telling of biblical stories and their meanings would indicate satisfactory achievement of the biblical content objective. (D) A quarterly home visit of each child would indicate adequate attainment of the goal of knowing the children and their families. (E) The receiving of one new child per quarter would indicate performance in the outreach goal. (F) One fellowship activity per quarter would indicate seriousness in group building.[3]

3. How will I do it? Planning and thinking ahead are necessary for any job, especially for methods to be used. Effective leaders and managers strongly encourage people to use the methods that fit their own personalities, experience, and gifts. In the case of inexperienced persons, leaders may mentor and coach the person in some

basic method, knowing that the sooner the person gains enough experience-based insight to graduate from the basic method, or at least adapt it, the more effective he or she is likely to be.

4. How am I doing? People need feedback on their performance, and they especially grow from the leader giving positive reinforcement when they are performing effectively or, early in their development, *almost* effectively. But, positive reinforcement is often badly done, with counterproductive results. A cartoon in the *New Yorker* once featured a rotund boss type, moving from person to person in an office pool, saying to one clerk at a desk, "Keep up the good work, whatever it is, whoever you are!" Positive reinforcement can be effective if we know our people, know their performance expectations, know what they are doing, and affirm specific behaviors and achievements. To know how people are doing and how to help them do better requires monitoring outcomes, giving frequent feedback, punctuated by more occasional (annual or twice annual) formal performance appraisal sessions.

Performance appraisal is the most utterly feared function of management. When an employee goes to the boss's office for the annual performance appraisal, a trapdoor to childhood memory snaps open and the employee walks in with all the old feelings that once accompanied being ushered into the principal's office. And, yet, people need to know how they are doing. For a church secretary or a parish visitor or a choir director or any other employee or volunteer, feedback is the breakfast of champions. Often, good performance needs positive reinforcement to stay on course; and sometimes a person's performance, like a pilot's, needs midcourse correction to get back on course.

Likewise, the typical manager dreads doing performance evaluations; some managers put off scheduling them almost forever—until the employee's performance is so bad and entrenched that termination may be the only option left. Yet, the responsibility for the organization's performance is ultimately leadership's. Leaders of organizations are employed to achieve the organization's objectives through other people, and very few people will find their initial orientation into a job sufficient to get on course and stay on course, without slippage or deviation, for the long term. Besides, as the organization's environment changes, the organization's mission and strategies should change, so the contribution that was needed from a particular role last year may not be exactly what is needed next year. So feedback on performance is essential in effective leadership.

Church leaders and their people are even more paranoid and obsessive about performance appraisal sessions than their counterparts in other organizations; yet positive reinforcement and midcourse corrections are even more needed in churches and church organizations, because church people often tend to "do their own thing" rather than pull together to achieve the church's mission. The need for performance feedback in a church is not confined to its staff; every voluntary leader and officer of every organization, and every person engaged in any kind of ministry or project, needs performance feedback to keep achieving or to achieve more.

Actually, much of the dread of performance appraisals is a symptom of another problem—fuzzy, or nonexistent, performance standards. When people's job descriptions and expected outcomes are not clear, the source of an appraisal may be the supervisor's subjective, but unspoken, expectations. For example, a nurse and her husband were leaving their community to go to seminary at Asbury. The nurse had managed for three years a staff of nurses on the fourth floor of a large hospital. In her exit interview with her supervisor, the supervisor praised her contribution saying, "You did exactly what I wanted you to do. You got all the nurses on your floor working together again." The nurse walked out of the interview in shock; her exit interview was the first time her supervisor had revealed that expectation of her performance. The nurse commented, in sharing this case, "I lucked out. If you bowl a strike and you haven't even seen the pins—you luck out!"

But, in contrast, when both manager and subordinate are clear about the job and its performance expectations, the worker already knows how she or he is doing. Clear performance standards eliminate the "surprises" from performance appraisals and liberate such sessions to become immensely productive. After my first performance evaluation with Joe Quillian at Perkins, I essentially took the lead in the subsequent annual reviews—based on the earlier goals set for the year.

There are several well-known "secrets" for effective performance appraisals: (A) Give your people frequent, informal feedback upon performance—so that there will be no new agendas or "surprises" in the more formal performance appraisal, but only a more structured conversation of matters already discussed informally. (B) Base the conversation upon performance in relation to the mutually agreed upon standards, outcomes, and indicators. (C) Use both the frequent informal conversations and the less frequent formal performance appraisals as opportunities to positively reinforce what the person is doing effectively. Where constructive critique is needed, do not focus upon or attack the person, but upon specific behaviors and their counterproductive effects upon the manager and/or the organization. (D) Lawrence Appley reminds us that "the main purpose of an appraisal of an individual should be to discover what can be done . . . to help him develop his greatest potential."[4] So, effective leaders do not use the performance appraisal primarily to dwell upon past performance, and especially past failures, but to learn from the past experience while focusing primarily upon the future and what the person will do to achieve objectives. (E) If termination, or placement in some other role, is very clearly warranted, a quick thorough incision is more humane and effective than cutting away inch by inch over time. Effective leaders do not try to make a subordinate's life miserable, hoping they will resign. They explain the reasons for the decision, they suggest the kind of job the person could do more effectively, they offer to facilitate the person's placement into a role that better fits his or her aptitude, and they give the person the opportunity to resign.

Another reason for learning to do appraisals well is to avoid the great discomfort and anxiety from doing them badly! Larry Knauff prescribes a basic strategy for performance appraisals:

1. Use the performance evaluation to discover *causes* of below standard performance. Use the early part of the interview for diagnosis, because underachievement is a symptom. Knauff has observed that, when someone is consistently performing below standard, one (or more) of five factors will be at the root of the problem. The manager may enter the interview asking five diagnostic questions: (A) Do they know, specifically, what *objectives* to be achieving? (B) Do they know *how* to do the activities to get those results? (C) Are they *capable* (mentally, physically) of doing the job? (D) Is the person *allowed* (by the organization, by circumstances, by herself) to do the job? (E) Does the person *want* to do the job? Knauff reports that, in 80 percent of the cases of underachievement, the cause is rooted in one of the first two questions. The cause is seldom rooted in the fifth; most people want to do their job effectively.

2. Generate, together, possible solutions to the performance problem, and then evaluate each possibility by criteria such as time, cost, and probability of success.

3. Make a decision regarding what will be done, by whom, and by when. Develop, together, a plan for implementation, and periodically monitor the progress of implementation.

4. Frequently people resist changes—even changes that can help them survive, achieve, and perform at their best. Knauff prescribes five strategies for dealing with such resistance which, when used as a package, will help about 95 percent of people to overcome their resistance and cooperate with a job-related change effort: (A) Let them understand the reason(s) for the proposed change. (B) Involve them in defining, conceptualizing, and developing the change. (C) Let them understand what they will gain if they change. (D) Let them understand what they won't lose if they change. (E) Let them understand what they will lose if they fail to change.

5. The outcome of a performance appraisal interview should be a development plan that, as implemented, will help the person achieve job objectives and move toward excellence. The person should be substantially involved in developing that plan, and the manager can especially facilitate its development by asking the person two questions: (A) What barriers in the organization, team, job, in yourself, or in your private life keep you from doing your best work? (B) What can I and/or the organization start doing, stop doing, do more of, do less of, or do differently to help you do your job better?

Chapter Nine: Why We Cannot Neglect Development, Controls, and Incentives

The supreme goal of Christian ministry is to develop people into the people they were born to be and deeply yearn to be. Christianity is entrusted with the Power that recreates the happy, effective, fulfilled disciples most useful to the Christian movement. In the development of people, Christianity may have less to learn from management than management has to learn from Christianity! It is said that Ted Turner once charged that Christianity is a religion for losers. Turner had grasped half of the truth. Christianity, at its best, understands, believes in, reaches, and develops "losers" into "winners"—the other half of the truth that escaped Turner's notice.

The church has long known to develop the identity and consciousness of its people through immersion in scripture, creeds, hymns, and liturgies. The church has developed a range of interventions for freeing and developing its people—from nurture, counseling, story-telling, and admonishing, to intercessory prayer, absolution, and exorcism, to experiences in fellowship, testifying, teaching, serving, and leading in Jesus' name. As in the case of eighteenth-century Methodism, the Christian movement has often engaged a disadvantaged and powerless people and transformed them into the salt, light, and leaven of their nations. Perhaps Christianity's greatest need today is a recovered confidence in the power of its tradition to change and develop people.

Nevertheless, the discipline of management reminds us that any leader who hopes to get things done through other people has a stake in the ongoing development of all the people who report to her or him, and management has much to teach us about doing that effectively. Indeed, Appley suggests that "a leader is measured by the extent to which he helps develop those under his direction."[1]

Several management methods for developing people are worth the church's attention; indeed, some churches already employ these methods:

1. Churches are increasingly using a *mentoring* method of helping new people into tasks, roles, and ministries. Frazer Memorial United Methodist Church, in Montgomery, Alabama, has all its people serve in one role or task for one calendar year. Each January, a person who has served in a role or task mentors his/her successor. In much of the world Church, mentoring facilitates the lifelong development of many disciples into productive and reproductive Christians. The maxim in management lore, "No one makes it without a mentor," is true of the church's history too. Church leaders have the special opportunity, today, to mentor ethnic minority people and women into the kind of achievers and leaders they were born with the potential and calling to be, and thereby model what this justice looks like to secular organizations and institutions.

2. Much of a person's continued development can be experienced from the feedback and planning that takes place in the process of *performance evaluation,* as delineated in the previous chapter.

3. The church is effectively adapting the secular world's model for developing people through various expressions of *formal*, experiential, high-commitment *training* events or series—from the Bethel Bible series or the Disciple Bible series to Parent Effectiveness seminars, to Marriage Enrichment weekends, to Willow Creek Contagious Christian evangelism seminars; but the church has barely tapped the potential for developing its people through formal training—particularly in light of the excellent training now available through video, audiocassette, and Internet resources.

4. Increasingly, churches are taking advantage of the kind of learning, insight, and new directions that can be experienced by importing a short-term specialist trainer or consultant.

5. Increasingly, churches are sending their people for intensive formal training experiences at the campuses of bellwether churches, denominational headquarters, or parachurch agencies.

6. We have learned from many organizations, including churches, that people learn and develop from experiences—especially if someone "processes" the experience with them to help them gain insight.

7. Many people experience development as a by-product of job enrichment, job enlargement, and tackling new responsibilities and challenges.

8. The special, and indispensable, function of leaders in organizations is to believe in what their people can achieve and to communicate, by language and body language, the expectation of achievement, thereby enabling "the self-fulfilling prophecy" to operate positively in the organization's culture.

At first blush, churches appear to have little in common with widget factories that must control costs to the cent and require their workers to "clock in" and "clock out." Furthermore, mainline Christianity rightly dissociates from the methods of cults that control the lives and minds of their people. The very word "control" can trigger pejorative connotations in our minds.

Yet, a well-managed, effective church will pay some appropriate attention to the control dimension of its organized life. For instance, faithful churches will control their expenditures. Faithful stewardship of resources requires that funds placed upon altars not be wasted, but be harnessed for the church's purposes. The "Praise the Lord" (PTL) scandal reminded all church leaders who value the church's credibility that honest and publicly accountable financial controls are good business for churches. The budget is an honest control mechanism that more church leaders need to understand and manage. Again, many churches have discovered that their effectiveness is tied to honest control of the time demands placed upon their staff and volunteer leaders, or to control of the year's schedule of activities, or to the control of meetings to make them efficient and productive.

Some churches are pioneering in various control activities. For instance, Frazer Memorial Church records the attendance of every person in worship every Sunday, and a team of volunteers feed each Sunday's worship attendance into a computer. Each Sunday the computer prints out the names of all members who have missed three successive Sundays. Team members telephone those persons, tell them they were missed, and ask if there is anything wrong; the people are visited that week if a visit is warranted. By that regular control mechanism, Frazer has consistently facilitated an average weekly worship attendance exceeding 60 percent of its membership—about double the average worship-attendance-to-membership ratio usually observed in very large mainline churches. Again, the staff of Highland Park United Methodist Church meets every

Monday and pores over the attendance reports of every Sunday school class and every organization for the previous week, identifying the indicators for determining where something good might be happening that deserves celebrating and, conversely, where an inquiry and possible intervention seems warranted. The philosophical foundation for appropriately controlling an organization and its activities is seen in Peter Drucker's helpful distinction between "controls" and "control":

> In the dictionary of social institutions the word "controls" is not the plural of the word "control." Not only do more controls not necessarily give more control, the two words, in the context of social institutions, have different meanings altogether. The synonyms for controls are measurement and information. The synonym for control is direction. Controls pertain to means, control to an end. Controls deal with facts, that is, with events of the past. Control deals with expectations, that is, with the future. Controls are analytical, concerned with what was and is. Control is normative and concerned with what ought to be. [2]

In that perspective, church leaders can readily perceive the desirability of controlling their church in the sense of staying on course, maintaining strategic direction, and not getting "out of control." That granted, the strategic usefulness of data about attendance, giving, expenditures, new members received, and so forth. become obviously useful controls to help a church discern its course, make strategic adjustments, and achieve its mission. The most indispensable type of control to institute is the goal setting connected with each major objective in the church's strategic plan, with periodic monitoring of goal-related achievement and the necessary adjustments and interventions to stay on course. To be specific, virtually the only large urban churches that are receiving significant numbers of new adult converts into their ranks are churches who: (a) set a specific goal, or "faith projection," for conversion growth; (b) regularly monitor the number being received in relation to their goal, (c) hold themselves accountable for reaching, with the Lord of the Harvest, their faith projection, and (d) make what-ever midcourse changes are necessary—such as visiting and inviting more pre-Christian people, starting new classes, or starting new ministries—to achieve their goal.

The greatest *incentives* connected with a congregation's mission are intrinsic to the work and its causes. Management technique can add no additional incentives to compare with the motivation that people experience from knowing that the Lord has visited them, and is using them, and they are called to be involved in the causes of the kingdom of God. The sense of being involved in a movement that, with Christ, seeks salvation, peace, and justice for all people fills people with a power and esprit than no other organization can match. Many people become followers of Jesus Christ through his church especially for the meaning and purpose they can experience from being involved in his holy work. Strategic churches are called to find and reach out to people in our communities who hunger for that kind of meaning and purpose, and thereby gather the most potent and reproductive harvest.

But even in the area of the church's greatest advantage, vis-à-vis other kinds of organizations, certain cues from management thinking can help inform our awareness and use of incentives: (1) We can involve people in the true work of the church rather than its counterfeit—mere routine "church work." Rummage sales and routine committee meetings do not engage people's deepest aspirations for meaning and purpose, and disillusioning involvement in "church work" may even immunize them against involvement in the true redemptive, reconciling, liberating work of the Christian movement. (2) We can, and must, pay church staff people what they are worth and not abuse their devotion to Christ and ministry. (3) We can, frequently, give public recognition for the people involved in ministries and find other ways to positively reinforce (and not take for granted) their contribution to the church's mission. (4) We can increase people's challenges and responsibilities as they are ready; and (5) We can provide many enjoyable and inspiring experiences for the people involved in the true work of Christ in the church and in the world. The church leader who really wants to achieve the church's mission goals through other people will always find abundant possibilities for helping that happen.

Mastering the Management Process

The church leader may readily forget many of the details and examples of this book and will, in time, read and reflect upon the management process and improve on what is written here. What the leader should not forget, but rather take pains to master and even "overlearn," are the eight questions that effective managers ask and the ten generic tasks or steps in the process of managing any organization. Generally, as organization leaders remember to ask all eight questions and attend to the ten tasks, their organizations are reasonably well managed. The major principles count most.

I have found it necessary to master these principles, and be able to recall them at will, so I invented an acronym to trigger my memory for recall at will: SAP-HOP-SADI! With that ludicrous acronym in mind, I can then recall "Situation Analysis and Planning, Organizing Human Resources, and Organizing Physical Resources, Standards of Performance, Appraisal of Performance, Development (and Controls), Incentives (and Rewards)."

Often as I gather interview data during a church growth consultation in a congregation, I recall the

SAP-HOP-SADI formula and find myself asking, "If this church gets to where it is going, where will it be? What are this church's greatest opportunities for reaching people today? What are this church's greatest strengths? Does this church have a strategic plan in place for their intended growth and achievements over the next five years? Do their people understand where this church is going, and why? What gifts and skills do the people have? How adequate are their facilities for worship? For Christian education? For parking? For fellowship gatherings? When people take a job here, how do they know what is expected of them? How do the leaders let people know how they are doing? How do the leaders help people do a more effective job? For what kinds of jobs do church leaders give public recognition, and how?"

In all known cases of churches growing less than they could be, the causes are multiple, but at least some of those causes are rooted in gaps in the management process: the leaders are not even asking one or more of the necessary questions, and they are neglecting (or are oblivious to) one or more of the essential tasks in the management of the church as an organization. Most often, (1) stagnant and declining churches lack an informed strategic plan for their future, and (2) people in various roles and jobs do not know what is expected of them and how their job fits into what the church is called to be and achieve.

Chapter Ten: The "Breakthrough Project" Way to Manage a Church Turnaround

Old Shiloh Church fulfilled all the worst stereotypes of a sluggish, declining, open country church. Over a thirty-year period, membership declined from 160 to 120, average worship attendance from 85 to 45. By 1990, 80 percent of the people present on any Sunday were members of the Crandall, Irwin, or Whiteman clans. (All but one of the church's leaders were from one of these clans; they did "let" an "outsider" work with the handful of junior high age kids.) People from the church membership's several other clans typically came for Easter, Christmas Eve, baptisms, weddings, and funerals. In the last twenty years, no one outside of the active and less active clans had joined the church by confession of faith; all eight, including the Irwin twins, were children being confirmed. Another half dozen people had married into one of the clans and joined by transfer, though none of those people were leaders and only two were regular attendees.

Any perceptive Sunday visitor to Shiloh would have noticed a hastily prepared Sunday school lesson, an unrehearsed choir anthem, a slightly adapted sermon originally preached (and published) by Clovis Chappel, a low level of energy, a lack of excitement, and no sense that Shiloh Church is a local branch of a movement with the vision and power to reach the world with Great News and New Life. In 1991, three things happened that changed Shiloh Church profoundly.

A tornado visited the church and deftly removed the steeple and pounded the outhouse beyond recognition. Ed Crandall, a carpenter, called a meeting of all the church's men and teenage boys. He invited another dozen men and boys who weren't in any church, but who had skills for what he had in mind. That night he challenged the group of thirty to repair the steeple and set it atop the church again, and to build a new ("two holer") outhouse and, "While we are at it, to repaint the whole church. And we need to do it all before the rainy season comes. That gives us two months of Saturdays. Can we do it?"

A planning committee met two nights that week and then telephoned assignments—who would bring what equipment, who would bring drinks and lunch, and so forth. For reasons not recorded, the planners decided that the first project would be the new outhouse, and they would do it in three weeks! Twenty people came the first Saturday, including several women who proved they could "hammer and paint as good as any man." Ed held up a work flowchart and explained who needed to do what in what order. He led a brief prayer and asked the Holy Spirit to be their unseen companion and to give them energy and unity. Someone knew some gospel choruses, and the work team sang much of the day as they worked.

Two unchurched men who worked that Saturday unilaterally brought their families to church on Sunday. The outhouse was finished in three weeks, then the steeple, and then some forty people administered two coats of white paint before the rains came. On the first rainy

Sunday, the attendance was seventy; four unchurched families were now involved, and two previously inactive member families. The choir had not sung better in years, "Preacher Tuttle" preached a new sermon that gripped both him and the people. People were so inspired that Tuttle almost gave an invitation as the service closed, but he "chickened out."

Several weeks later, Ed Crandall's wife, Margaret (Shiloh Church's "resident saint"), experienced an aneurysm, followed by a stroke. Her physician said she would not likely live long—weeks at most. Margaret said she wanted to die at home, with her family and her people, where she could see her church from her bedroom window. A woman, Edith Richmond, who had served on Ed Crandall's work team, had observed how Ed organized that project. She called a meeting, asked for volunteers, and organized what became the church's lay ministries to Margaret, Ed, and their kids.

For the five weeks that Margaret lived, laypeople brought them food every day; teams of two laypeople, including two new Christians, would take turns spending the day with the Crandalls—supporting them, running errands, transporting kids to Little League practice, and so forth. Through it all, Margaret's spirit was caring and triumphant, and people who came felt that she ministered to them! Several laypeople who were ministering to the Crandalls started ministering to other people in the community and inviting people to church. Margaret Crandall's funeral was the only "standing room only" service within anyone's memory.

The next week, a distressed Mrs. Irwin telephoned Preacher Tuttle. One of her sixteen-year-old twins, Martha, was pregnant. She was not married, and the fellow who had said he loved her had departed for parts unknown. Martha was clear that, though the baby was unplanned, she wanted it to live, and she wanted to try to raise it. But the family, Mrs. Irwin said, felt over-whelmed with a hundred questions: Should they keep the baby? If so, what should they do next? What do we do with Martha's guilt and depression? How would their family face the shame in that closed, traditional community? How do you raise a child with this stigma? The pastor's wife, Diane Tuttle, shared this story as a prayer concern in a meeting of her women's circle. Spontaneously, the circle of seven women voted to "adopt" Martha and her family. One circle member, who had retired early from social work, said "I can help Martha and her family clarify all of their options, and I can help them plan life from this point on." Several other women thought of ways to help, from making baby clothes to recruiting baby furniture, and thought of other people in the community who could help. Edith Richmond worked out a plan on paper to make sure all the bases were covered.

Two weeks after the baby girl's birth, Martha and her parents presented her before the Shiloh congregation for Tuttle to baptize into the Family of Faith. The baby was given the name Margaret, in honor of the memory of Margaret Crandall. In his baptismal remarks, Tuttle referred to the Christian movement's "secret weapon" for raising kids: "We provide a community where kids know they are more wanted and loved here than any-where else, and we covenant together to help each other raise our kids." That afternoon, sixty women crowded into the large family room of a new Christian family to have a shower for Martha's baby. That was the day that Preacher Tuttle decided to remain as pastor of Shiloh Church for the rest of his life, God and the bishop will-ing. "This was the only church I ever served where I saw my people becoming The Church!"

By now old Shiloh Church was experiencing momen-tum, and the place was becoming contagious. The leaders now deeply believed in what God can do through his people, and they started dreaming bigger dreams and even planning the church's future. They noticed that no church in the county had a ministry to deaf people, so they hired a person to sign the services. They invited every deaf person, and his or her family, to come to Shiloh Church. If they said "no," Shiloh's people kept inviting and, in time, they developed other ministries for deaf people and their families.

A leader observed that over half the families in the church had one or more family members struggling in the grips of addiction. Someone proposed that the Holy Spirit might be greater than the power of addiction; they found the right people to lead Twelve Step recovery groups for people addicted to alcohol, narcotics, and gambling, and in time two dozen people were in recovery.

By 1995, Preacher Tuttle had earned enough credibility that the leaders supported his idea of starting a second worship service for seekers with contemporary music and a small band! By 1998, Shiloh's attendance was exceeding 250, their membership was pushing 400, they expanded their paved parking lot, and 10 to 20 people a year were now joining their ranks as converts from the world. The church was now considering other "radical" ideas—such as every person being in a small group and every Christian being deployed in ministry. They planned to plant a new church in another community in the county and to involve dozens of their people each year in short-term mission experiences overseas. They did confess some trade-offs and some mixed feelings about how things were going. They might have to add a third worship service, with maybe three concurrent sessions of the Sunday school. If "Old Shiloh" kept growing beyond that capacity, they'd have to build another church!

The discerning reader will have noticed that Shiloh Church moved "from tradition to mission" through the catalytic experience of a series of "projects," namely, the building project following the tornado, the organized response to Margaret Crandall's critical illness, the organized response to Martha Irwin's pregnancy, and others. Over twenty-five years of studying churches, I have observed this pattern frequently. In fact, the Shiloh Church case study is a semifictional account informed by about twenty such cases, though the Shiloh case is not extreme but rather typical, more or less the kind of renewal that hundreds of churches have experienced and a hundred thousand could experience. The purpose of this chapter is to convince you that the way out of stagnation and the way forward for your church could be the "Breakthrough Project Strategy."

A "project," as the dictionary suggests, is "an organized undertaking." Other typical features of projects in effective churches include:

1. An effective project, typically, takes a limited period of time, weeks (or months at most), to achieve the project's objectives.

2. A project usually requires special "promotion" among the members, or the target population, or the supporting constituency.

3. To achieve the project's objectives, the church usually needs to devote priority deployment of resources (human, financial, or physical) for the duration of the project.

4. The project frequently requires the close orchestration of the services of many people with different gifts necessary to the projects' success.

115

✳ 5. The achievement of a good project is usually visible and is publicly celebrated.

I have observed, in churches that have experienced
turnaround through projects, that the projects typically
become the milestones that shape the church's identity.
Often, as in Shiloh's case, the first project is often an
organized response to a crisis and, as in Shiloh's case, the
first project builds or improves the church's physical
facilities. But, as in Shiloh's case, the next projects in the
series focused on achieving something special in ministry for people and for God—such as "when our kids
painted homes in Appalachia" or "when we sponsored a
Leighton Ford crusade and filled the high school audito-
rium" or "when we started the Big Brothers program" or
"when we took a busload of guys, half of them
unchurched, to Promise Keepers" or "when the special
campaign got the children's hospital paid for" or "when
we started our contemporary worship service." They
define themselves in terms of what has been achieved,
and what they yet plan to achieve.

By contrast, the identity of stagnant and declining
churches may also be historically shaped—but in much
more institutional and ecclesiastical terms, such as "the
years Reverend Smith was pastor" or "the time our
church hosted the district meeting" or "the period when
Sally McKinney served as the conference Women's president" or "the decade when we paid our apportionments
to the denomination, 100 percent." Typically, stagnant
churches have had few important projects over the years
that were visibly achieved in measurable time, or they
haven't allowed such experiences to define their identity.

Stagnant and declining churches also often define
themselves in terms of the church's activities; they are
beehives of activities that are expected to go on forever,

which wind down long after most people have forgotten what they were supposed to achieve. These churches are so busy in "good church work" that they never really get around to the work of the church. Occasionally, stagnant churches may have a great idea, but they do not manage the project effectively enough to achieve its goals; this failure inoculates them against acting on other great ideas. On the whole, project-oriented churches are more effective, with more satisfied members, and experience more growth than activity-oriented churches.

The project strategy to achieving things was not, of course, invented in our time, though we probably invented the language to explain it. Many leaders and movements of the past have prospered from it.

John Wesley frequently took a project approach to his leadership of early Methodism, and much that eighteenth-century Methodism achieved was achieved through visible, promoted, prioritized projects. Very early in the movement, Wesley marshaled the support and resources needed to build the New Room in Bristol, Methodism's first church building. Soon thereafter, Wesley campaigned and organized for the building of a school for colliers' children at Kingswood, where the movement first surfaced in one of England's most destitute communities. The Kingswood school was not yet paid for when the building was finished, so Wesley kept promoting! Sometimes a great need or crisis called forth a concerted project, as in the severe winter of 1740–41, when Wesley organized collections to ensure that the poorest members had sufficient food and heat for the winter. Most of Wesley's publishing ventures were managed as projects—with an obsessional series of promotions, between 1749 and 1755, to publish his Christian Library. But the Christian Library, to furnish poor people with excellent books of manageable cost and length, illustrates that many of Wesley's projects were stepping stones toward larger objectives. The building of the Foundry in London, and of Wesley's chapel late in his career, were occasions for rallying and focusing the spirits of the Methodist people.

Many Christian leaders seem to know, intuitively, that periodic achievements give a necessary "shot in the arm" to the movement, so they organize and promote projects—to keep spirits up and people involved, and to maintain momentum. The place of projects in church effectiveness is a timely consideration, because 80 percent or so of America's 360,000 Protestant congregations are "stagnant" or declining—not growing, not notably vital, and not achieving the church's goals—if, indeed, they have conscious goals. These churches do not experience much achievement beyond routine "church work." Their members lack the satisfaction of being part of a contagious, growing, achieving movement. Few visitors read from the body language of such churches that this is the Community of the Messiah, whose people taste the life of the Kingdom, whose mission offers the hope of the entire human race. How do such churches achieve a turnaround? How do they become what they were called to be? How do they begin to realize their destiny and achieve their mission?

The usual answers—change pastors, try a new program, work harder, pray more, schedule a week-long revival or a renewal weekend—do not usually make much difference. The process of "strategic planning," which we outlined in a previous chapter, has a good track record. In this process, the leaders, with other interested people, study the church to identify its strengths and weaknesses, and they study the community to identify the threats and opportunities, upon which they define their mission and its objectives, and then the broad strategies that can move them toward their objectives, and the more specific programs and activities to achieve the objectives.

Every church that can do strategic planning should do strategic planning. There are no good reasons not to, and there is no more proven approach to the future than to plan your work and then work your plan. Page Smith, a social historian who studies social movements, observes that "The leader with a system, however inadequate it may ultimately turn out to be, is at a vast advantage over a systemless rival, however brilliant." Strategic Planning may be a universal law of church growth. I have not yet found a church that had a strategic plan in place that was informed, had wide ownership, and was being diligently implemented, that was not growing.

Many churches are experiencing turnaround, new life, and growth through strategic planning. But strategic planning presupposes an ingredient in churches that, often, is not present: It presupposes that the church is already healthy enough, with enough self-esteem, to risk a revealing "diagnosis" that would expose its weaknesses. Furthermore, strategic planning presupposes that the congregation already faces the future with confidence and assumes they can make a difference. Prior to the tornado, Shiloh Church was not secure enough to submit to the vulnerability of looking at its weaknesses and at the threats posed by a changing community, and they were aware of no reasons to face the future with apostolic confidence. The leaders who were not in denial about their record of decline would have assumed continued decline, with the agenda of perpetuating the past as long as possible. Many churches, like Shiloh, are not self-confident enough to risk a diagnosis, or confident enough of the future to devote a season to strategic planning.

How can insecure, low self-esteem churches experience renaissance and become achieving churches? Until recent years, we had no model with obvious promise. We observed that effective growing churches have many projects, but we had not yet understood the project orientation to be a strategy for effectiveness and growth; and we hadn't guessed that projects could be a strong key to the turnaround of declining congregations. But Robert Schaffer, fortified by a doctorate in psychology from Columbia University and the experience of a career of consulting with organizations, has pioneered an approach to achieving organization turnaround that has obvious relevance for many churches. The approach he identified is not foreign to church experience, but rather describes a natural process by which many orga-niza-tions (including congregations, like Shiloh) have risen from stagnation to new momentum, a process that is even more effective when, unlike Shiloh, the strategy is conscious and its execution is intentional. Before Schaffer's book, *The Breakthrough Strategy: Using Short-Term Successes to Build the High Performance Organization* was published by Harper & Row in 1988, you had to track down his writings in an astonishing variety of pub-lications, from *Harvard Business Review* to *The Christian Science Monitor* to *Modern Healthcare* to *Plastics World*, to gain knowledge of his insights. Fortunately, his most essential insights can be cogently summarized.

Schaffer counsels change agents to troubled organiza-tions against, for now, any diagnostic activities. Looking at the weaknesses of an organization that is not ready for that only depresses the organization and arouses and intensifies the very forces ("restraining forces") stacked against the changes the organization needs. But, Schaffer's extensive research and experience would per-suade us that pathological organizations are never as unhealthy and hopeless as appearances suggest. Indeed,

> In any situation, no matter how many problems exist, no matter how many gaps and weaknesses in the people and the systems, no matter how many conditions beyond the control of management are impeding progress, it is almost always possi-ble to identify one or two specific short-term bottom-line goals

for which the ingredients for success are in place or could be readily marshaled.[1]

Furthermore, in such organizations a focus on specific goals and results will motivate action more than focusing on problems or grand designs. The experience of one or more successful projects will help the organization to feel more competent. The way forward is through aiming at tough-but-attainable objectives and should take place in groups, where individuals publicly contribute their ideas to what is being considered, commit themselves to the objectives, and feel ownership in the emerging projects.

In *The Breakthrough Strategy,* Schaffer develops his case through three contentions. First, most organizations, most of the time, are working at only 40 percent to 50 percent of their actual potential. (If you grant that Christianity is really supposed to be about the mission and ministry of the laity, then most churches are achieving at, say, 10 percent of their potential.)

Second, most organizations, like Shiloh Church, have had crisis experiences in which the organization's people focused their energy, harnessed their abilities, and pulled together to achieve something great in very measurable time. The crisis catalyzed an extraordinary effort and achievement because of what Schaffer calls the "Zest Factor." In chapter four of *The Breakthrough Strategy,* Schaffer unpacks the components of the Zest Factor, which explains why a crisis can "stimulate radically higher performance":

- Sense of urgency
- A challenge
- Success near and clear
- People collaborate—a new "esprit"
- Pride of achievement
- Fear of failure

- Exciting, novel, like a game
- People experiment and ignore "red tape"

Despite the excitement and fulfillment that people experience from achievement in the wake of a crisis, Schaffer observes that after the crisis was over, the organization's achievement pattern recedes back to "normal." It doesn't occur to leaders that what the organization achieved in the crisis was "normal," and they invent rationalizations for returning to business as usual, that is, the achievement pace would burn people out or keep the organization in a perpetual state of crisis.

Third, Schaffer disagrees. He believes that the Zest Factors breathe life and satisfaction into work. Most important, Schaffer contends that a project orientation to the organization's renewal and work can contribute may of the Zest Factors without the burnout and other things that people fear.

As suggested, a project is a planned undertaking that has a definite end. When finished, it is perceived as finished and achieved. That is, projects are not the usual ongoing ministries or programs (like Sunday school or women's circles) or special ongoing ministries or programs (such as a weekly thrift shop or a weekday day-care ministry). When a project is achieved, the orga-nization moves on to other things—at least for the time being. A project may involve the painting of a pensioner's home, the production of a musical, the building of a family life center, a summer work project in Appalachia or Kenya, or a thousand other possibilities.

Organizations effectively achieve projects through project management, which became a somewhat distinct discipline in the 1960s when leaders began tackling very complex projects—like the launching of a satellite, requiring the competencies and contributions of many different persons and the orchestrated scheduling of their many interdependent actions. Sophisticated "Gantt Chart" and "PERT Chart" approaches were developed for the planning and management of projects. Being in (but not entirely of) their culture, churches are increasingly taking a project approach toward some of their objectives.

Project management is, essentially, the practice of leadership and management focused on a specific project—so the insights in this book apply to project management and do not have to be reinvented for this chapter. Nevertheless, project management is a specific type of management that has its own distinct challenge, and requires some specific skills. For instance, project management requires a project manager (not usually the pastor), who, in collaboration with a team of people representing the organizations and skills the project will need to succeed, engages in the following activities:

1. They define the project's *objectives,* and the periodic *milestones* toward achieving the objectives, and the *scheduling* of each milestone's achievement.

2. They divide the project into *tasks,* and *subtasks,* and define *who* will need to achieve each task by when.

3. They determine and allocate the *resources*—the personnel, time, funds, and facilities that will be needed for each task and for the completed project. (Experienced project managers anticipate that some tasks will take longer, or cost more, than first anticipated, so their plan provides some "cushion.")

4. Once the project is underway, they periodically *monitor* the progress of the project, to perceive problems and engage in interventions or midcourse corrections.

5. Throughout the project, they are reminding everyone of the objectives of the project and *com-*

municating its progress to each work unit and to the church. This communication is usually amplified by the use of visual *charts* that enable the planning, monitoring, and wider communicating.

Unless a crisis (like Shiloh Church's tornado) forces a project upon a church, how would the church's leaders choose an initial project to get some momentum going? Schaffer's advice would be to choose a project the people are already ready for. "Exploit existing readiness—don't try to create new readiness."[2] Many savvy pastors and other staff leaders have discovered this principle in their own way. The arriving new pastor interviews all of the church's leaders and key stakeholders, asking, "What really needs to be done? If you were given unilateral power to change one thing around here, what would it be?" The new pastor almost invariably discovers "an unorganized consensus" around some things the people believe need doing, some of which make good sense and would advanced Christ's work. So this pastor discovers which way the parade wants to go. Then he runs around and gets in front of it and raises his baton and starts marching, because he is supposed to be the leader!

Typically, after the church has achieved several items on the people's agenda, the church has new momentum and self-confidence, the pastor is now owned by the people as "our pastor," and the church is now more open to the pastor's ideas. This principle illustrates that, in a church or any other organization, there are no "unmotivated" people, although there may indeed be people who are not yet motivated to move with someone else's great idea. There are things that even the "least motivated" people would like to see done. Why not begin there?

Schaffer, throughout his writings, also emphasizes several other *criteria* for a leader group's selection of a breakthrough project:

1. Consider beginning with an urgent and compelling goal.

2. Consider choosing a project that is achievable in a relatively short period of time—thirty to sixty days maximum.

3. If the project will take longer, choose a first-step sub-goal that can be achieved in thirty to sixty days.

4. Choose a project that expresses what people are ready, willing, and able to do.

5. Choose a project for which the resources and authority for achieving it are already available. Many churches (and other organizations) wring their hands over what they cannot do, and ignore what they can do!

6. Choose a project that, when achieved, would be a clear and visible success, breaking the hand-wringing syndrome.

7. With the momentum of several successes, and *Snowball effect* the people's increasing confidence and competence, take on larger projects.

8. Choose projects that would advance the long-range objectives of the organization, as those become defined.

9. In time, with increased congregational self-esteem, the leaders will want to put their project orientation more clearly within the service of a strategic plan.

Dr. Schaffer is confident that, no matter how many problems or deficiencies an organization has, "there are at any given time a great many opportunities for fresh, short-range successes. These opportunities can be translated at once into some actual achievement without first diagnosing the organization's 'ills' or otherwise reforming or changing the organization or its people."[3]

Through breakthrough projects, Schaffer believes, organizations can "make miracles routine." [4]

Schaffer has thus observed, and helped, organizations to gain strength by a series of projects, most of which are discrete steps toward achievement of longer term objectives (in someone's mind!). Within the experience of a series of achievements, the organization's people will gain in competency and group self-esteem. Later, with raised self-esteem, the people will be more open to analysis or riskier interventions—if still needed. As an organization is experiencing achievement (and probably not without it), the people increase in their ability to identify development needs and to work on problems.

Schaffer delineates several generic "steps" that any organization can follow in the development of a breakthrough project:

1. Put aside, for now, problems and things that cannot be done. Identify things that can be done, for which there is readiness in the people.

2. When a project is chosen, identify its specific, attainable, and measurable goals, stressing the specific results desired.

3. Develop a *schedule*, with a *project work plan*, specifying names, steps, and dates—who will do what by when, and who will report to whom.

4. Periodically monitor the progress of the project, evaluate the progress, give help where necessary, make necessary changes and midcourse corrections. ✗ *Clarify*

It is crucial for the organization's development, Schaffer believes, for the leaders to use each project success to educate the organization and the organization's capability to take on challenges and opportunities; to plan and execute the projects that will increase its success more and more. The most important discipline within this strategy is to *process* what the organization is learning. This involves blocking out the time, during and after the project, to talk about what we did and how. What did we do that contributed to our success? What would we do differently next time? It is important to *record* those insights, report them in board meetings, and pass them on to the next generation of leaders. *Calculate*

Schaffer observes that the most successful organizations use breakthrough projects to produce "new skills and insights into how to organize, set in motion, and maintain control over bigger, tougher, and more numerous projects." The most important phase of any project is for its participants to recall, reflect upon, rehearse, and record what they have learned from each successful, or unsuccessful, project. They thereby generate insights and internalize new skills, they write them down, they rehearse and refer to them before launching the next project. In time, the church has produced new, experientially based, widely owned, and demonstratively productive "norms" for "the way we do things around here." Through many processed projects, the church's "culture" experiences change. *Calculate*

Robert Schaffer's breakthrough project research and consulting experience has witnessed remarkable changes in the culture and psychology of many organizations. They have proved to themselves that "we can do something." They now know how to achieve as a group. They have established some new norms for how they achieve together. They have "broken through" their previously limited perception of what is possible for them to achieve. The breakthrough project approach has brought renewal and greater effectiveness to a wide range of organizations, from major industries to small companies, from health care organizations to Bell Canada.

But, is the breakthrough project approach valid for significant numbers of local churches and other church organizations? Yes. Although the hypothesis had not occurred to me until I discovered Schaffer's writings, my studies of "turnaround churches" concludes that the pattern and causes of turnaround fit the breakthrough project model even more often than the strategic planning model. When this model becomes more widely known and consciously employed, its effectiveness will be widespread indeed.

I have observed projects used by churches with three different agendas. First, some projects are a one-time challenge, never to be repeated—such as a relocation or a new facility or a Billy Graham crusade or a disaster relief project. Second, some projects are designed to get something started that is intended to have a long life— like starting a second worship service, or a Twelve Step recovery group ministry. Third, some projects prove to be annual projects— such as a vacation Bible school or an annual December exhibit of the expressions of Christian themes by local artists.

Churches do not typically experience much recovery and new growth from one project, but rather through a series of achieved projects. Though later projects are typically ministry focused, a church's first breakthrough project usually involves the people pulling together with their hands and funds to improve their physical facility

128

—a specific, visible achievement that communicates to others their intention to stay in the community and contribute to its life, and communicates to the church that "we can do it."

For instance, when an arsonist destroyed the building of the Highlands United Methodist Church in Jacksonville, Florida, this two hundred-member church faced plans for a new sanctuary, offices, and Sunday school rooms that would cost them $170,000. The pastor, Jack Hileman, helped the people face questions like "Who are we as a people of God?" "Where are we headed?" "Do we have faith in ourselves only, or in God's claim upon us?" He reports that "we decided our days of growth . . . may now begin again." From that missional decision, they decided to build again. But "project financing worried our blue-collar membership most, and it is this concern which brought a definite response to the third question. In one pledge meeting we completely underwrote the project debt. Members surprised themselves! This became for all of us tangible proof of both God's claim upon us and the strength of our fellowship."

The Lake Panasoffkee United Methodist Church, also in Florida, saw the need to relocate and build again, and the project excited and mobilized the people. The pastor, John Barham, reports that "a major factor underlying many of the exciting things happening here is long-term vision and specific goal setting. Once the decision was made to relocate and rebuild to reach Lake Panasoffkee for Christ, a new enthusiasm was realized as each specific objective (goal) was reached. Large, insurmountable tasks are broken unto manageable steps to be conquered by the power of Jesus—one by one."

Dr. Rose Sims, whose first career was in higher education, served as pastor of the United Methodist Church in Trilby, Florida, for seven years. Through the threefold strategy of ministry to pre-Christian people, relational evangelism, and a series of projects—some one-time projects and some ongoing projects—she helped bring renaissance to the fourth "nearly closed" country church she pastored. One September, when no pastor could be found, she volunteered to serve this "tiny unpainted church with a rusty mildewed tin roof," as she described it, in an area of Central Florida's greatest poverty. With support from the larger United Methodist Temple in Lakeland, Trilby Church invested $1,400 and three working Saturdays to wash and paint the roof and to administer three coats of white paint to the rest of the church. In time they added a new steeple, and a church bell began to ring again. They began food and service ministries to the poor people of the area. Some 250 people attended a Harvest Festival celebration. The church now overflowed, and an architect, moved by what was happening, volunteered plans for a new sanctuary, kitchen, and rest rooms. They renovated the parsonage, then gave it to house their emerging ministry to migrant farming families. They negotiated a $14,000 grant from the Florida United Methodist Conference and attracted $210,000 in federal funds! They erected a new church sign:

TRILBY UNITED METHODIST MISSION
and
FARM WORKERS SELF-HELP, INC.
An Ecumenical Outreach in Jesus' Name to All God's
Children in Need

In Rose Sims's seven years as pastor, Trilby built a new church, grew in membership from 62 to 309, grew in average worship attendance from 28 to 160, and received 232 people as new Christians. This marvelous story, and many of its lessons, are featured in Rose Sims's two books—*New Life for Dying Churches! It Can Happen*

Anywhere (New Life Church, 1992), and *The Little Church That Could* (New Life Church, 1996). She believes that the pastor's greatest leadership opportunity is to help the people believe that God can achieve great things through them and that God can reach people through them. She believes, with William Temple, that "the Church is the only society on earth that exists for its non-members." She advises the rising generation of church leaders that "the main thing is to keep the main thing the main thing."

As mentioned, many churches achieve renewal and growth through one or more annual projects. If learning is processed, successful annual projects significantly equip a church with group skills for achievement, and typically they interact with other features of congregational life to impact people's lives in many different ways.

I have, for decades, observed an outstanding example of such an annual project in the Hopewell United Methodist Church, an open country church several miles outside of metropolitan Downington, Pennsylvania. It was founded in 1783 as Battens Chapel, and Francis Asbury preached there many times. By the 1950s, Hopewell Church was a fairly typical, struggling, open country church of 150 members; some members doubted the church's future viability. A high school English teacher and playwright, Charles J. Ax, had attended Germany's Oberammergau Passion Play, and he dreamed of writing a version of the Passion Play that could be produced by a local church. He wrote the play, and Hopewell Church first performed it in their social hall on Palm Sunday of 1963. To the writer and cast's astonishment, that first "bed sheet and bathrobe production," performed by a cast of thirty, was crowded to "standing room only." They scheduled two additional performances to handle the demand, and a tradition was born. The next year, six performances were sold out.

By 1966 the cast had doubled and was being publicized as "The Hilltoppers." Taking advantage of a slope on the church's back property, the church constructed an amphitheater seating about one thousand people. Many adults and children of the church and community labored "as though they were possessed" for twenty-five months to construct it! A local banker loaned the church $5,000 for materials, and became so involved in the church's vision that he provided the collateral for the loan. People with landscaping knowledge and other skills volunteered their time and energy; some were church members and some not (yet). The plans they implemented were excellent and elaborate. One man, Frank Dietz, did the research to assure that the costuming would be authentic, while other people were involved in the installation of 60,000 feet of underground wiring. The first weekend in the amphitheater, the play was performed for more than three thousand people. By 1973, the Passion Play was produced nine times over three weekends. Hopewell's people see signs that the Spirit is with them in this project. Marian Smith, who keeps the project's records, reports that the play has been rained out only fourteen times in its history; for sins not yet publicly revealed, four of the rainouts occurred in 1985!

By the summer of 1998, more than 225,000 people had seen Hopewell Church's Passion Play. People come from hundreds of miles away, many in bus delegations. Some churches schedule their confirmation classes to climax with a pilgrimage to the Passion Play. Some persons hear the gospel, and see it dramatized by people like themselves, for the first time in their lives. The production has become more elaborate—with an expanded script and seventeen scenes. The story begins with the raising of Lazarus, but there are flashbacks to earlier events and teachings of the Gospels before the events leading to Christ's crucifixion. The first cast of thirty people has grown more than tenfold. The play has gained in dramatic realism. During a scene in one performance, a woman sitting close to the procession to Calvary hit a Roman soldier, played by Harry Bryant, with her umbrella. (By the time the "oral tradition" embellished the story, she had hit Pontius Pilate!)

One of the church's agendas for the Passion Play is to involve many people in the total project, especially all new members. Every person is involved in some role consistent with his or her gifts and interests—from acting, to directing, to stage crew, to make up, to costumes, to refreshments, to publicity, to finances, to ushering and traffic control. The play now has three casts; each cast performs once each weekend for three successive weekends in June. Many people have joined this church who might not have joined another, because the play engaged their imaginations, and their subsequent involvement in the project engages their talents and interests and lets them express it for God. They feel useful and find purpose through this project. Many people devote decades to the project as their Christian avocation. Alice Bryant, the current producer, has been involved for thirty-three years. All three young men who now play the Christus grew up in the church and with the Passion Play as part of their lives.

Understandably, lives are changed as people get this involved with the gospel story, as they rehearse it for months, year after year, and as they experience communicating the Passion Play's message to others. As our society becomes increasingly secular, people become Christians almost never from one single experience, but from a chain of experiences over time, usually months. Hopewell's Passion Play provides links in that chain for countless people. Many people have attended the play and became more receptive to the gospel; other people who were already seekers have attended and stepped over the line in that season; other people, already Christians, have become more deeply convinced, committed, and rooted in their faith. Many members, including children and youth, know the biblically based script more or less by heart. People's lives sometimes change directions. A young art teacher, who played the role of Mary of Bethany for several years, took a sabbatical to work with inner-city children in Philadelphia. Another teacher, who played the role of Peter for years and then played the Christ, broadened his appreciation of the church's "regular" ministries, and he chaired the church's administrative board.

The church has experienced fairly sustained growth for thirty-five years. Its location still gives it no "natural" church growth advantages (except a slope for an amphitheater!). It is still an open-country church, located on an obscure county road. Until a housing estate (Asbury Village) was built near the church in one direction, there was little civilization within view. The church is still relatively hard to find. The leaders often ask new members, "How did you find Hopewell?" Much of the growth was experienced in the twenty-six-year pastorate of Donald Bower, who died from a brain tumor in 1982. His widow, Joyce Bower, has remained with the church through the years and is now director of the Passion Play. Today, Hopewell United Methodist Church is one of the largest open-country churches in North America, with an active membership approaching 1,100, with three worship services combining for more than 500 in attendance each weekend. It draws regular attendees from a radius of ten to fifteen miles. The growth of the church is not adequately reflected in that data, because of population mobility, deaths, and so forth. More than

3,000 people have joined this open-country congregation since the Passion Play was launched.

Two pastors serving Hopewell Church in the 1980s, Gerald Crowell and Mike Carr, once confessed that the church is not devoid of problems. Indeed, they observed, one would reasonably expect some turbulence from importing all of those "artistic temperaments"! But the members bring with them an awesome range of skills, and "energy, warmth, and a willingness to innovate." Crowell and Carr reported that the enduring Passion Play project "is the glue that holds the congregation together, the magnet that attracts many new people, and the catalyst that involves and changes people." The church experienced new growth in the 1990s; by 1998, Hopewell Church had outgrown its new facility built in 1990. The people regard their Passion Play as an expression of the congregation's mission, but their vision for mission does not stop with the summer production. The church now gives more money to world mission than any other church in the Eastern Pennsylvania Conference of The United Methodist Church.

Charles Ax, the originator of the dream and the writer of the script, also acted in the play every year until his death in 1979. He once confessed to *Together* magazine that he was the only actor who frequently forgot his lines. "But," he added, "I can ad lib my way out!" Naturally, the introduction of a breakthrough project requires an advocate with an idea—like Charles Ax. (Then it requires a project manager—who may not be the same person.)

Robert Schaffer would remind us of certain factors in the change agent's role: The leader in this role needs to educate the other leaders and stakeholders and sell them on the possibility and methodology. The change agent will need to help the organization in the choice of a breakthrough project. In most churches, the advocate will introduce the realism that one project does not usually turn the organization around to stay, that lasting turnaround requires a series of projects, and within some plan. The change agent holds out the reasonable promise that the congregation will become a more achieving organization and will develop its people, will gather momentum and achieve its purpose by building on one small achievement after another. Schaffer claims that "channeling the readiness that exists in virtually every organization into immediate, rewarding, and skill expanding achievement lays a foundation for subsequent, more ambitious steps. Then exploiting these new opportunities sets in motion a sustaining process of improvement and development."[5]

Appendix:
The Hunter Congregational Health Questionnaire

You are invited to participate in a study that will identify your church's strengths and opportunities and will help the church become more effective in its mission and ministries. Please begin by sharing the following personal data.

Name of your church:

_____

Your gender: Female ( )   Male ( )

Your "generation": Born before 1924   ( )
                    Born between 1925 and 1942 ( )
                    Born between 1943 and 1960 ( )
                    Born between 1961 and 1981 ( )
                    Born since 1981   ( )

Your time in this church:
                    More than twenty-five years ( )
                    More than ten years   ( )
                    Two to ten years   ( )
                    Less than two years   ( )
                    Nonactive, or former, member ( )

Thanks. Now, please read the following sixty-four statements and, using the scale below, decide the *degree* to which you disagree or agree with each statement. Write the appropriate number, from 1 to 6, in the parenthesis following each statement.

Strongly Disagree	Disagree	Disagree Somewhat	Agree Somewhat	Agree	Strongly Agree
1	2	3	4	5	6

Feel free to write in any explanatory comments.

A. *Correspondence to the Profile of "Effective Organizations"*

1. This church has a very clear mission or *purpose.* Everyone in the church knows and owns this mission, and it drives the church's priorities, decisions, and activities. (   )

2. This church's direction for the years ahead is clear. We have an informed *strategic plan* in place that the people own and is being implemented. (   )

3. Our leaders study the trends, changes, and needs of people in the wider community that the church serves. We often respond and *adapt* to changes in this wider community by offering new ministries and programs. (   )

4. Most of the church's important decisions and plans are not made in isolation or at the top. Everyone who has a stake in the church's future gets *involved* in the decision making, problem solving, and planning that shapes our church's future. (   )

Strongly Disagree	Disagree	Disagree Somewhat	Agree Somewhat	Agree	Strongly Agree
1	2	3	4	5	6

5. The church's people are clear, and in agreement, about the *values*, beliefs, and convictions that should be the foundation for the church's life and ministries. ( )

6. Our church's policies and practices are *consistent* with what we say we believe and value. ( )

7. In this church's services, ministries, and programs, we strive for *excellence* by continuously looking for ways to improve. ( )

8. We have very *high expectations* for members in this church, not only in matters like attendance and giving, but even more in matters like lay ministries and outreach to pre-Christian people. ( )

B. *Correspondence to the Profile of "Apostolic Congregations"*

9. Our church's leaders deeply believe that this church is *called* by God *to reach* one or more unchurched pre-Christian populations. That is this church's main business. ( )

10. Our church is persistent, and often effective, in rooting people meaningfully in *scripture*. Many of our people really know the Bible. ( )

11. Our people are earnest in *prayer*, and they expect and experience God's presence, and power, in their lives and ministries. ( )

Strongly Disagree	Disagree	Disagree Somewhat	Agree Somewhat	Agree	Strongly Agree
1	2	3	4	5	6

12. Our church likes, understands, wants, and has *compassion* for lost, unchurched, pre-Christian people. ( )

13. We feature at least one weekly worship service, at a time convenient to unchurched people, that uses the language, style, and music that fits the *culture* of some unreached population in the church's ministry area. ( )

14. This church has a high priority for involving everyone in *small groups.* ( )

15. This church has a high priority for involving everyone in *lay ministries.* ( )

16. The members of this church receive regular (at least quarterly) *pastoral care.* ( )

17. This church engages in many *ministries* to unchurched pre-Christian people. ( )

18. This church's leaders are driven by a *vision* of what a tremendous positive difference second birth and becoming a Christian disciple will make in any person's life. ( )

C. *Correspondence to Church Growth Principles*

19. The pastor and the people really *want* this church to grow. ( )

Strongly Disagree	Disagree	Disagree Somewhat	Agree Somewhat	Agree	Strongly Agree
1	2	3	4	5	6

20. The pastor and the people are willing to devote whatever time, money, or energy it takes to help this church grow. (   )

21. This church's leaders and people believe that the Gospel is contagious and that many unchurched people in the ministry area are *receptive*. (   )

22. We have ways of *identifying* unchurched people who are likely to be receptive, and we find ways to reach out to them. (   )

23. Our church has at least one user-friendly, *culturally relevant worship service* every weekend that we would love for our unchurched friends to experience. (   )

24. This church does not assign all of the *evangelism* ministry to the pastor. Many of our people often converse with unchurched people in the community about the faith and invite people to involvement with Christ and the church. (   )

25. This church's members often invite people in their kinship or friendship *networks* to visit, become involved, or follow Christ. (   )

26. We often start *new* classes and other groups as recruiting groups and ports of entry for seekers and new people. (   )

27. We often start *new ministries* that minister to the needs of pre-Christian people. (   )

Strongly Disagree	Disagree	Disagree Somewhat	Agree Somewhat	Agree	Strongly Agree
1	2	3	4	5	6

28. We identify, recruit, and develop enough *leaders* to do all that God calls this church to do in ministries. ( )

29. This church *identifies* with and is involved in the struggles of unchurched, pre-Christian, and "hard living" people in our community. ( )

30. This church is regularly involved in the planting of *new churches.* ( )

31. This church identifies with the struggles of the world's peoples and strongly supports *foreign mission.* ( )

D. *The "Climate" in the Church for Encouraging Outreach and Growth*

32. The leaders appreciate and recognize the members who serve in committee roles, church offices, and official leadership roles. ( )

33. The leaders appreciate and recognize members who engage in ministries to persons, such as Sunday school teachers, small group leaders, and hospital visitors. ( )

34. The leaders appreciate and recognize the members who help bring new people into the faith and church. ( )

35. We have a clear sense of our *identity* and mission as a denomination. ( )

Strongly Disagree	Disagree	Disagree Somewhat	Agree Somewhat	Agree	Strongly Agree
1	2	3	4	5	6

36. The *music* in this church is easy and enjoyable to sing, as well as inspiring. (   )

37. The preaching and teaching are biblically rooted and expressed in the people's *language*. (   )

38. In recent memory, at least one *worship* service has been exciting and moving, with a sense of God's presence. (   )

39. A number of people in this church *experience*, or want to experience, the grace of God, and there are opportunities to talk about, seek, and share such Christian experience. (   )

E. *The Congregation's Leadership and Management Dynamics*

40. This church's *purposes* and goals are clear to most people. (   )

41. For the most part, our church's organizational *structure* does not get in the way, but it helps us accomplish our mission. (   )

42. Our church's *facilities* and equipment are adequate for achieving our purposes in the future, or will be. (   )

43. Our church's *budget* reflects what we say are our purposes and priorities. (   )

Strongly Disagree	Disagree	Disagree Somewhat	Agree Somewhat	Agree	Strongly Agree
1	2	3	4	5	6

44. We identify people's *gifts* and strengths, and we build ministries, projects, and jobs around these; we do not try to force "square pegs into round holes." ( )

45. In programs, *who* is responsible for doing *what* by *when* is usually clear at all levels. ( )

46. When you accept a ministry, task, or job in this church, you know what to do and for what *outcomes* to work. ( )

47. When you accept a ministry, task, or job, you receive the *training,* coaching, and support that enable you to develop your competence and confidence to do it well. ( )

48. We give people *feedback* on their performance in tasks and ministries, both "ataboys" and suggestions. ( )

49. Ministries, tasks, and jobs are distributed to enough volunteers that few people experience *burnout.* ( )

50. This church, in an average week, has more volunteers working more hours in service, ministry, and outreach than in meetings, chores, and institutional maintenance. ( )

F. *Human Relations Dynamics in the Church*

51. The church's leaders and members like, enjoy, and trust each other. ( )

Strongly Disagree	Disagree	Disagree Somewhat	Agree Somewhat	Agree	Strongly Agree
1	2	3	4	5	6

52. New people who join or visit are warmly welcomed, and they feel wanted and included in the life and fellowship. (   )

53. There are relatively few rules and regulations around here, and the ones we have are necessary for the church to achieve its ministry goals. (   )

54. Faithfulness, excellence, and creativity are rewarded more than passivity, conformity, and "going along." (   )

55. Openness and honesty, in personal relationships and in spiritual matters, are encouraged, affirmed, and valued much more than pretense or "faking it." (   )

56. When there is a conflict of ideas or feelings, people feel they are heard and conflicts are faced and resolved with goodwill. (   )

57. When there is a problem, the leaders and the people do not look for who to blame; they look for ways to help and for what the church can learn from the experience. (   )

58. In this church, people matter much more than budgets, buildings, and traditions, and people who are not yet Christian disciples matter even more. (   )

G. *Orientation to the Future and to Change*

59. This church is much more interested in effective ministry than in perpetuating traditions. (   )

Strongly Disagree	Disagree	Disagree Somewhat	Agree Somewhat	Agree	Strongly Agree
1	2	3	4	5	6

60. Many of the ways in which we "do church" are very different than how it was done traditionally, like in the old country or during the 1950s. (   )

61. In significant ways, our thinking is not confined to inherited assumptions, patterns, and goals. We *think* differently about the world around us, and what it means to be the Church and to be in ministry, than we did a generation ago, or even a decade ago. (   )

62. We are very open, in this church, to making any changes that would help us both keep the faith and more effectively reach and disciple people. (   )

63. We are not obsessed with perpetuating "the good old days." We are confident that our church's best days are, or can be, ahead of us. (   )

64. In this church, we are taking on challenges so large that we will only succeed if we pull together and God is with us. (   )

Notes

1. Why Any Church Leader Needs to Know the Principles of Management

1. This data was faxed to me by request from the Yoido Central Full Gospel Church in June 1998. For more information on the Yoido church's home cell strategy, see Paul Yonggi Cho's books *Successful Home Cell Groups* (Plainfield, N.J.: Logos International, 1981), and *More Than Numbers* (Waco, Texas: Word Books, 1984).

2. From Lawrence A. Appley's *Formula for Success: A Core Concept of Management* (New York: AMACOM, 1974), p. 1.

3. From George S. Odiorne, *Management and the Activity Trap* (New York: Harper & Row, 1974).

4. From Paul Hersey and Kenneth H. Blanchard, *Management of Organizational Behavior: Utilizing Human Resources.* Seventh Edition (Upper Saddle River, N.J.: Prentice Hall, 1996), p. 7. The writers explain that this definition does not specify business or industrial organizations. Management, as defined, applies to organizations whether they are businesses, educational institutions, hospitals, political or military organizations, or even families. The achievement of organizational objectives through leadership is management. Thus everyone is a manager in at least certain activities.

5. The term "groups" refers, here, to all ongoing groups, large and small, in which membership is meaningful and in which the members minister to each other—such as Sunday school classes, women's circles, men's fellowships, youth groups, Bible study groups, home cell groups, Scout troops, and so forth.

6. Lyle F. Schaller, *Growing Plans* (Nashville: Abingdon Press, 1983), pp. 93-94.

7. Carl F. George, *How to Break Growth Barriers: Capturing Overlooked Opportunities for Church Growth* (Grand Rapids, Mich.: Baker Book House, 1993), chapter 6.

8. Ibid., ch. 9.

9. Ibid., ch. 10.
10. Ibid., ch. 11.

2. A Defense of Management to Its "Spiritual Despisers"

1. Leander Keck, lecture, summer 1997, East Ohio (UMC) Pastor's School.

2. See FitzSimon Allison, *The Cruelty of Heresy: An Affirmation of Christian Orthodoxy* (Harrisburg, Pa.: Morehouse Publishing, 1994), pp. 27-28.

3 There are parallel cases to this twofold competence in many other expressions of ministry. For instance, the effective preacher knows both public communication theory and homiletics. The effective counselor knows psychology and the literature of pastoral care. You would want the designer of your new facility to know architecture and church architecture.

4. Warren Bennis and Burt Nanus, *Leaders: The Strategies of Taking Charge,* Second Edition (New York: HarperBusiness), pp. 19-20.

5. Hersey and Blanchard, in *Management of Organizational Behavior: Utilizing Human Resources,* Seventh Edition (Upper Saddle River, N.J.: Prentice Hall, 1996), p. 7, offer a similar distinction between leadership and management. "Leadership is a broader concept than management. Management is a special kind of leadership in which the achievement of organizational goals is paramount. The key difference between the two, therefore, lies in the term *organizational goals.* Leadership occurs whenever one person attempts to influence the behavior of an individual [or] group, regardless of the reason. It may be for one's own goals or for the goals of others, and these goals may or may not be congruent with organizational goals."

6. Bennis, p. 20.

7. This article is reprinted in J. Thomas Wren, ed. *Leaders' Companion: Insights on Leadership Through the Ages* (The Free Press, 1995), pp. 114-23.

8. Ken Blanchard, "Turning the Organizational Pyramid Upside Down," in Frances Hesselbein, Marshall Goldsmith, and Richard Beckhard, eds., *The Leader of the Future: New Visions, Strategies, and Practice in the Next Era* (Jossey-Bass Publishers, 1996), pp. 81-82.

4. The Management Perspective: Roots, Questions, Tasks

1. From Lawrence A. Appley's *Formula for Success: A Core Concept of Management* (New York: AMACOM, 1974), p. 3.

2. The Management Course of the AMA is offered in four one-week units in many major cities of the U.S. and in several other countries.

3. (New York: AMACOM, 1974).
4. Appley, Formula for Success, p. ix.
5. Ibid., pp. 1-2.
6. Ibid., p. 1.
7. Ibid., p. 7

5. Situation Analysis for the Local Church

1. Robert H. Waterman, Jr., *The Renewal Factor: How to Best Get and Keep the Competitive Edge* (New York: Bantam, 1987), p. 103.
2. Ibid., p. 111.
3. See Lynn and Bill Hybels, *Rediscovering Church: The Story and Vision of Willow Creek Community Church* (Grand Rapids, Mich.: Zondervan Publishing House, 1995), chapter 3.
4. See John C. Condon and Fathi Yousef, *Introduction to Intercultural Communication* (Indianapolis: Bobbs-Merrill, 1975).
5. David Burnett, *Clash of Worlds* (Nashville: Thomas Nelson, 1992), chapter 2, "Exploring Other Worlds."
6. See Ezra Earl Jones's *Strategies for New Churches* (New York: Harper & Row, 1976), chapter 3.
7. George G. Hunter III, *To Spread the Power: Church Growth in the Wesleyan Spirit* (Nashville; Abingdon Press, 1987), chapter 8.
8. Jones, *Strategies for New Churches*, pp. 42-43.
9. See pages 194-97 of *To Spread the Power* for a more complete development of the rationale for "membership strength" and for an expanded discussion of useful indicators of membership strength.
10. For much more on social movements and the role of membership strength within them, see Ralph H. Turner and Lewis M. Killian, *Collective Behavior*, Second Edition (Englewood Cliffs, N.J.: Prentice-Hall, 1972), part 4.
11. Lawrence A. Appley, *Formula for Success: A Core Concept of Management* (New York: AMACOM, 1974), p. 34.

6. Strategic Planning for Church Growth

1. Donald A. McGavran, *Understanding Church Growth*, Second Edition (Grand Rapids, Mich.: William B. Eerdman's Publishing, 1980), pp. 440-41.
2. George G. Hunter III, *To Spread the Power: Church Growth in the Wesleyan Spirit* (Nashville: Abingdon Press, 1987), pp. 186-87.
3 Lyle E. Schaller, *Create Your Own Future!* (Nashville: Abingdon Press, 1991).
4. Ibid., p. 40.
5. Ibid., p. 40.
6. Ibid., p. 42, adapted.
7. Lawrence A. Appley, *Formula for Success: A Core Concept of Management* (New York: AMACOM, 1974), p. 35.

8. Ibid.

9. James C. Collins and Jerry I. Porras, *Built to Last: Successful Habits of Visionary Companies* (New York: Harper Business, 1994).

10. See Hunter, *To Spread the Power*, chapters 3-7, for a fuller delineation of these three strategic principles.

11. Ibid., pp. 76-86.

12. Donald A. McGavran, *The Bridges of God* (New York: Friendship Press, 1955).

13. See Win Arn and Charles Arn, *The Master's Plan for Making Disciples* (Pasadena: Church Growth Press, 1982), p. 43.

14. For a comprehensive introduction to strategic thinking for all kinds of organizations, see Henry Mintzberg and James Brian Quinn, *The Strategy Process: Concepts, Contexts, and Cases*, Third Edition (Upper Saddle River, N.J.: Prentice-Hall, 1996).

7. Organizing People and Resources to Achieve the Church's Apostolic Purpose

1. For instance, Bishop Richard Wilke's *And Are We Yet Alive?*, William H. Willimon and Robert Wilson, *Rekindling the Flame*, and Douglas W. Johnson and Alan K. Waltz, *Facts and Possibilities: An Agenda for The United Methodist Church*, all three published by Abingdon Press.

2. See C. Peter Wagner, *Your Spiritual Gifts Can Help Your Church Grow* (Glendale, Calif.: Regal, 1979) and Kenneth Kinghorn, *Discovering Your Spiritual Gifts* (Grand Rapids, Mich.: Zondervan, 1986).

3. Lawrence A. Appley, *Formula for Success: A Core Concept of Management* (New York: AMACOM, 1974), p. 41, emphasis added.

8. Delegating Kingdom Work to the People of God

1. Lawrence A. Appley, *Formula for Success: A Core Concept of Management* (New York: AMACOM, 1974), p. 43.

2. Ibid., p. 73.

3. Knauff's third question—"How well should I do?"—indicating a performance range between a minimum acceptable level of performance and the maximum probable level is, I think, less appropriate to churches than companies, factories, sales organizations, and so forth. Inclusion of this dimension would, in any case, unnecessarily complicate the process of developing performance standards in a church not yet used to developing and using standards at all.

4. Appley, *Formula for Success*, pp. 78-79.

9. Why We Cannot Neglect Development, Controls, and Incentives

1. Lawrence A. Appley, *Formula for Success: A Core Concept of Management* (New York: AMACOM, 1974), p. 88.

2. See Drucker's *Management: Tasks, Responsibilities, Practices* (New York: Harper & Row, 1973), p. 494, and all of chapter 39.

10. The "Breakthrough Project" Way to Manage a Church Turnaround

1. Robert Schaffer, "Make Success the Building Block," in *Management Review,* August 1981, p. 49.

2. Robert Schaffer, *The Breakthrough Strategy: Using Short-Term Successes to Build the High Performance Organization* (New York: Harper & Row, 1988), pp. 71-73.

3. Robert Schaffer, "Management Development Through Management Achievement," in *Personnel,* May-June 1972, p. 31.

4. Schaffer, *The Breakthrough Strategy,* p. 4.

5. Schaffer, "Management Development Through Management Achievement," p. 32.

Index